Knockaloe
Insel Man

be Kasse mit Genehmigung der zuständigen Behörden.

Isle of Man

The Postal History of

20th Century Internment Mail

A catalogue of postal markings on mail to and from
the Internment Camps on the Isle of Man with valuations;
including details of postal stationery, postcards, artwork, maps,
paper currency and information about the various camps.

by

Bernard Osborne

The Isle of Man Postal History Society

2015

Published by The Isle of Man Postal History Society

iomphs@manx.net

Copyright Bernard Osborne and
The Isle of Man Postal History Society

First published 2015

ISBN 978-0-9934052-0-4

British Cataloguing in Publication Data
A catalogue record for this book is available from the British Library

Printed and bound by Gomer Press Limited, Ceredigion

The Isle of Man Postal History Society
A member society of the Isle of Man Philatelic Federation

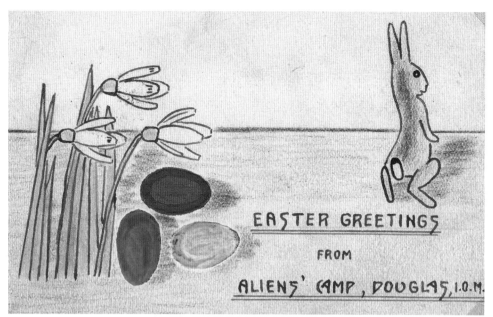
WW1 Internee hand drawn Easter Greetings postcard.

WW1 Photographic postcard of Internee Actors in Knockaloe.

WW2 photograph showing guards at entrance to Peveril Camp. Private Collection.

Contents

Foreword

As the President of the Isle of Man Postal History Society it is my privilege and honour to write this foreword to the Society's first ever published book on the Isle of Man Postal History of 20th Century Internment Mail incorporating related Banknotes, Maps and Postcards. Whether you are reading this book as a collector of this interesting aspect of Manx Postal History or as a person seeking information on the Isle of Man Internment Camps during the First and Second World Wars, then this publication will bring to you many aspects hitherto unpublished.

The Isle of Man Postal History Society was formed in 1973, just after the Isle of Man gained its postal independence on the 5th July and ever since, whether by its published bi-annual philatelic bulletins or monthly Society meetings, it has striven to identify and increase the knowledge on all philatelic aspects of the Isle of Man, whether current or past. It was through these endeavours that the proposal to fully research and publish a book on the philatelic history of the Isle of Man Internment Camps was raised in 2007, under initially my predecessors the late Dr. Ron Conti and latterly the late Barry Wilson, and commenced. Without the dedication and enthusiasm of Bernard Osborne, the current Hon. Secretary of the Society, this book would never have come to fruition and the Society will always be grateful to him. It is my pleasure to record the Society's debt to the late John Greenwood for his assistance with this publication and additionally, as mentioned elsewhere, the Society owes its appreciation to all those people who have assisted in any way, large or small, to this publication.

As a forerunner to this publication on the 8th August 2011 the Isle of Man Post Office issued eight stamps and a further four within a Miniature Sheet to commemorate the Postal History of Knockaloe Internment Camp. Along with Mannin Collections Limited, I provided the source material for the issue and its background research. These stamps complement the material depicted within this book and illustrate their philatelic use.

With this being the 100th Anniversary of the commencement of the Great or First World War on the 28th July 1914 and ceasing with the Armistice on the 11th November 1918, it is fitting that this publication is published within this period in 2015 to commemorate the 100th Anniversary of the Knockaloe Post Office. It is the only such post office within the First or Second World Wars that was a fully functional post office operated by the British Post Office and as such it illustrates the upheaval to many tens of thousands of civilian aliens caught up in the conflict and interned in the Isle of Man. The Society hopes that this publication will be of interest not only to the philatelic historian but to all people who have an interest in Manx History during what was such a turbulent time in the affairs of the World.

It is hoped that this publication will lead to new discoveries being brought to the attention of the Society in due course.

Kerry J. Kemp

Hon. President

Isle of Man Postal History Society

Introduction

The postal history of internment mail with its associated cachets was first highlighted in a series of short publications by J. B. Leece and R. Ward, followed in 1981 in the catalogue of Dr J. T. Whitney and in 1989 a catalogue by Charles Field. (References to Field's catalogue numbers are from "Internment Mail of the Isle of Man" by Charles Field). Over the years the Bulletin of the Isle of Man Postal History Society has published updates of the information outlined in these publications sourced from study groups and information sent to the editor by members of the Society. It became clear that it would be of value for all the material thus gathered to be made available in a more up to date book.

In earlier catalogues variants of a given mark have sometimes been noted, or not, sometimes in very general terms, also some marks have been described but no illustration of these have been shown. This catalogue has more detailed descriptions of such varieties and illustrations of marks which have so far been unavailable have been included wherever possible. It is recognised that in the future new discoveries may be made and the numbering system used has omitted numbers so that in future editions of this work new material may be included without renumbering marks already catalogued.

It has been mentioned that members of the Isle of Man Postal History Society, Mannin Collections Limited and others have been of great help in compiling this catalogue and special thanks must go to the following people. Local members Ron Henry, Kerry Kemp, the Basil Wood Collection, Ron Conti, John Perkins, Peter Bonbernard, John Greenwood and Algy Massy together with overseas members Graham Gleeson and Kurt Pantele. Paul Weatherall, Alan Franklin and their colleagues at the library of Manx National Heritage and staff at the Isle of Man Registry have also been of considerable assistance. The Society is grateful that permission has been given by Manx National Heritage and the Isle of Man Registry together with other contributors to publish marks and documents in their collections or archives. Thanks to Maxine Cannon, Manager of the Isle of Man Philatelic Bureau, and also to Clare Bryan and members of the Society who have proof read this work and added valued suggestions. Finally to Martin Davies for all his help in producing the final version of this book for processing by the printers, Gomer Press.

An outline map of the Isle of Man showing the location of Internment Camps in
the First and Second World Wars marked in red and blue respectively.

Prisoner of War Study Price Codes

It should be noted that the valuations are only a guide to possible auction prices for a single strike on a cover or postcard. Multiple strikes or ones on scarce postcards, registered or other items may command higher prices, and poor or incomplete ones, or ones on items in distressed condition, much lower ones. It will be likely that retail or insurance values will be higher than those given and will vary quite considerably. Whilst the values given are regarded as realistic at the time of publication, and to a certain extent reflect rarity, as time goes by they will need to be adjusted to take account of market trends and the value of sterling. The society will from time to time publish amendments to this list when required. Where a wide price range is indicated, it reflects that, for example, a mark where only two are known a higher price will be commanded than if ten are known but the mark will still be regarded as extremely rare.

Code	Price range	Code	Price range
A	Up to £15	I	£150-200
B	£15-20	J	£200-250
C	£20-30	K	£250-300
D	£30-40	L	£300-400
E	£40-50	M	£400-500
F	£50-80	N	£500-750
G	£80-120	O	£750-1000
H	£120-150	P	Over £1000

Abbreviations used

U	Unrecorded	m/s	Manuscript	ps	Postal stationery
?	Unknown	hex	Hexagonal	cds	Counter date stamp
Sim	Similar	N/A	Not applicable	perf	Perforations
Bx	Boxed	IOM	Isle of Man	D	Douglas
Lg	Large	cvr	Cover	K	Knockaloe (Peel)
d/o	Double oval	lbl	Label	M	Mooragh (Ramsey)
t/o	Triple oval	cat	Catalogue	P	Peveril (Peel)
s/c	Single circle	d/c	Double circle	pc	Postcard
R	Rushen (South)	pg	Page	off	Office
oct	Octagonal	h/s	Hand stamp	ppc	Picture postcard

Layout

Where possible illustrations of items described are shown together with the Isle of Man Postal Society number allocated. It should be noted that they may not be exactly to scale and some are hand drawn in which case fine detail may be slightly different from the original. It should also be noted that where items illustrated are in colour, shades may not be exactly the same as the original.

Postmarks and other items are listed in columns as shown here.

1st Column Postal History Society reference number. This is a new listing and should not be confused with the numbers given by Whitney or Field in their catalogues. The numbers used by them may be found in the appendix of this publication. Numbers are not always consecutive so that new discoveries can be added in future without disruption to the numbering system. Items from the First World War start with 1 and the Second World War with a 2 or 3.

2nd Column Date of use. Where only one item has been shown to the editor the year date is given if not already noted by Whitney. (Field does not quote date of use but only the opening and closure of the camp). In some cases the earliest date of use noted by Whitney has been amended to take account of new discoveries.

3rd Column A brief description of the mark or item together with wording and size if appropriate together with any other relevant information.

4th Column The colour or colours of the mark or item. Detailed varieties or shades of colour has not been attempted.

5th Column The letter code for the price of the mark or item. This gives a price range for the mark or item in good condition that might be expected at auction. Marks on piece will be at least one price range lower. Retail prices will often be higher than the prices given, especially when of outstanding appearance.

The final section of the publication is devoted to postcards, various postal history items, banknotes, maps of camps from various sources and recent stamps issued by Isle of Man Post related to internment. Those illustrated are not intended to give a definitive list but are shown to give an example of a range of material available.

An internee produced greetings card from Onchan Camp.

CORRESPONDENCE OF PRISONERS OF WAR IN DETENTION CAMPS.

1. Prisoners of War are only allowed to write two letters a week, unless special leave is granted, which will only be given under special circumstances. Letters will be sent out from this Camp at   and

2. Letters must be written distinctly in ink, and, if possible, in English ; they must not exceed in length two pages of writing paper. Writing paper will be supplied to the prisoners. Writing between lines is prohibited Prisoners are not allowed to stamp envelopes themselves.

3. Letters to prisoners which are indistinctly written or are more than two pages in length will be subjected to considerable delay. Prisoners, therefore, are advised to request their correspondents to write short, distinct letters. Letters of unusual length will not be delivered. Where several letters are addressed to one recipient, one or more of such letters may be detained.

4. All letters to or from prisoners must contain the full name and address and number of the sender on the back of the envelope, otherwise they will not be delivered.

5. Letters to and from prisoners of war must be restricted entirely to private and business affairs. The mention of political affairs, as well as naval and military operations, is prohibited. Should any letters contain any such reference, they will be withheld and destroyed without the prisoner being informed.

6. Should any concealed news be conveyed in letters to and from prisoners of war, the prisoners concerned are liable to be deprived of their privilege to write and receive letters.

7. Anyone writing more than two letters a week will have his correspondence destroyed.

8. No correspondence allowed on Post Cards.

9. Photograph Post Cards must only bear Name and Number of sender.

10. No correspondence allowed to or from Prisoners of War.

11. Only one letter to be written on one day, i.e., each writing day.

12. No newspaper cuttings allowed.

C. & F.—1,000.—8/15.

Official regulations relating to mail in WWI.

The Knockaloe Website and Visitors Centre

100 years ago, on 17 November 1914, over 23,000 internees, such as Josef Pilates, together with their guards, including Archibald Knox, started moving into Knockaloe Farm, Patrick Village.

100 years later, a registered charity company limited by guarantee has been set up by the community of Patrick Village to utilise the 150 year old Patrick Village School building to develop an on-site Visitors Centre, with a web based Archive, to bring this very human aspect of Patrick Village and Isle of Man history to life.

Phase 1: The Website and Archive – now launched

As few records of Knockaloe Camp and its residents remain, the Charity is using the latest technology to collate the lost stories of the internees, guards and village members, by reaching out to their descendants around the globe, via the internet, 100 years later. As the fragments of information provided both from descendants and various other sources gradually overlap more and more, this will allow the Charity to rebuild the records which were sadly destroyed, but more importantly to try to understand the impact upon the real lives of those people and their families, and to tell their story 100 years later. Anyone with any information about any aspect of Knockaloe and Patrick village life will be encouraged to contribute to an ever growing archive of this time, the people and the families involved.

Bringing this information together will allow descendants to find out more about what happened to family members, as well as allowing us to tell the story about this little known aspect of the First World War.

www.knockaloe.im was launched on 17 November 2014, 100 years to the day after the first internees moved into Knockaloe. The Charity commemorated this centenary by moving its first internee onto the website on that day. Since launching, the Charity has received many more stories as well as various other information which is being collated into our Archive on a daily basis.

Phase 2: The Visitors Centre – under development

Situated in 150 year old Patrick Village School, a historic village building located opposite the entrance to the site of Knockaloe Camp, with views over the entire Camp area, the Visitors Centre will seek to tell the story of what happened in our village 100 years ago to today's visitors of all ages, from both on and off the Island, in a visual and imaginative way.

It will seek to help visitors understand what it would have been like at that time, through a virtual tour with digital reconstructions, imagery, letters and artefacts and ultimately through physical hut reconstructions. But it will also focus on helping visitors find out more about any specific former residents, internees and guards or share their stories with us. As many of the internees were German, Austrian and Turkish, it will be multilingual.

A few features and remains of the Camp and its inhabitants can be seen in the village and on Knockaloe Farm, and from the Visitors Centre a self-guided walk will aim to help visitors visualise how the camp would have looked (using technology via an "app" to provide visual reconstructions), identify points of interest, including the remaining internee graves, and to pinpoint hut locations.

To find out more, to tell us your family's story or help us in any way please visit www.knockaloe.im   or contact us by e mail: info@knockaloe.im
Keep up to date via our facebook page at
www.facebook.com/knockaloeinternmentcampiom

Funding the Project

Part of the project involves renovating the 150 year old Patrick Village Schoolrooms, a historic building situated at the entrance to the camp and itself in desperate need of repair.

The Charity has already raised a substantial sum from the community for the website and part of the renovation, but it has much more yet to raise over coming months and all support would be gratefully received.

The registered charity is seeking donations from Trusts and individuals and is looking to develop internee descendant "friends" to help support the renovation and development costs of this project.

The Charity

The Charity is run by members of the community, including professionals and those already running visitor attractions on the Island, who are donating their experience to ensure its professionalism, integrity and success of this venture. The Visitors Centre provides a future for the Schoolrooms which is vital for this central building to Patrick community life. It also brings to life the story of a unique village history and the people it involved.

The First World War

Douglas and Knockaloe

The PC Single Circle used on Douglas and Knockaloe items

The venue of application of the PC mark has come in for some discussion. It has long been thought that the mark was applied in the U.K. possibly by postal censors in Liverpool or elsewhere. There is some evidence that some may have been applied in the Isle of Man as covers used within the Island have been seen which bear this mark. It could of course be argued that they travelled to Liverpool to receive the mark and then back to the Island for delivery. Examples of these marks have been seen on items dated 1919 as the camps were not emptied until well after the armistice on 11th November 1918 and continued in use until late summer 1919 at Knockaloe and late March or early April 1919 at Douglas.

Most outgoing mail from both Douglas Camp and Knockaloe received a cancellation of a single circle enclosing the letters PC. Incoming mail may also have a single circle PC mark applied. In earlier publications on Prisoner of War mail of the Isle of Man the only mark illustrated show the words POST FREE / PRISONERS OF WAR within the rim of the circle. Recent discoveries show that marks were used without that wording, and at least three varieties of this mark have been recorded of either 30mm, 34mm or 36mm usually on incoming mail. It was already known that a range of colours was used for the PC marks but it has become clear that, not surprisingly, a range of slightly different types of the PC mark exist, with or without stars which can be of differing sizes, the size of the single circle can vary as can the size and shape of dots between the PC letters.

The following is not a definitive list but gives examples of some of the varieties of the PC mark found. Unfortunately not all covers seen have a date of use applied so it is not possible to give an exact date of use of every mark, in which case the date of 1914 has been given. Where only one example has been found the year of use has been given (if known) together with its colour. The values given are for a single good mark on a plain cover or tuck-in postal stationery item without any other cachet or printed camp markings.

100	1914	POST FREE / P.C./ PRISONERS OF WAR s/c with round dots and stars 33mm			Red/black violet/ pink	C
101	1914	POST FREE / P.C./ PRISONERS OF WAR s/c with square dots and stars 34mm			Red/black violet/ pink	C
102	1914	POST FREE / P.C./ PRISONERS OF WAR s/c with one square right dot and stars 34mm			Red/black violet/pink	C
103	1914	POST FREE / P.C./ PRISONERS OF WAR s/c with square dots but with left star 35mm			Red/black violet/pink	D
104	1916	POST FREE / P.C./ PRISONERS OF WAR s/c without dots but with stars 35mm			Red/black violet	D
105	1917	P.C.	s/c 30mm	No stars	Red/black Blue/black	D
106	1919	P.C.	s/c 30mm	No stars, square dots	Black/red violet	D
107	1919	P.C.	s/c 34mm	One left star	Violet	D
108	1917	P.C.	s/c 36mm	Lg. Stars	Black	D

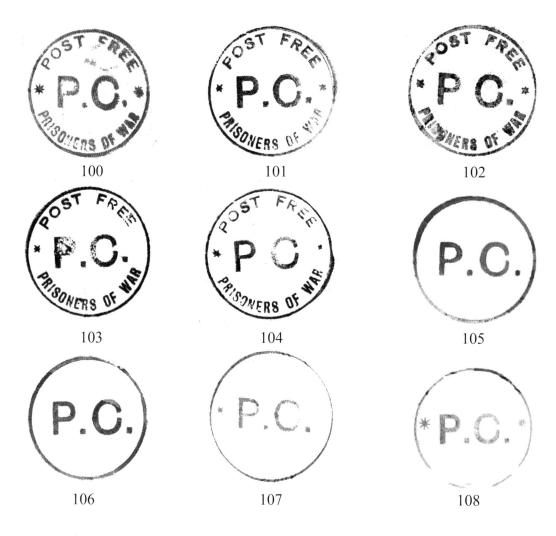

100   101   102

103   104   105

106   107   108

Global Postal Stationery and Censor Labels

This applies to such items which have no printed camp cachets. Values are for used items without any other marks. Mint items command lower prices.

110	1914	Prisoner of War / bx No/ Stamp/ Required on envelope, various papers and sizes.	Black on white	C
111	1914	Prisoner of War / Pat 2333/15/bx No/ Stamp/ Required	Black on white	C
112	1914	Prisoner of War / bx No/ Stamp/ Required/ NICHT HIER SCHREIBEN! on entire tuck-in various papers & sizes with printed lines on reverse	Black on white	C
113	1915	OHMS envelope printed with camp name	Black	G
114	1915	Registered envelope various sizes with camp markings	Blue on buff	L

Censor labels on covers

115	1916	OPENED BY / CENSOR	Black on white	C
116	1917	G. Royal Arms R.	Black on white	C

Prisoners of War.

No
Stamp
Required

Herrn

Aug. Künzle

Sportshaus

Arosa

Schweiz.

Kanton Graubünden.

110

Prisoners of War.
(Pat. 2333/15).

NO
STAMP
REQUIRED.

Herrn 1622 8.VI.B Capt 4 Comp 1 Knockaloe Peel I.o.Man.

Miss

Nellie Harf.

Tailors 1 High Street.

England.

Ongar. Essex.

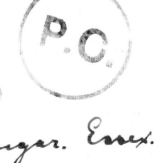

P.C.

111

NICHT HIER SCHREIBEN!

112

113 / 129

114

OPENED BY CENSOR.

P.W. 85

115

(B21865.) Wt. W 752—17. 100m. 10/17. **Gp. 135.** S. & S., Ltd.

116

Private mail without camp marks used to Douglas or Knockaloe

Outgoing mail or incoming mail to internees without camp markings or an examiner label are usually valued at A or B depending on the arrival or departure location.

Douglas Camp

This camp was based at "Cunningham's Holiday Camp for Young Men" which came into use for internees on 22nd September 1914. It was situated at the top of the cliff above Little Switzerland overlooking Douglas Bay. It housed some 3300 internees who were divided into three main groups, the Ordinary Camp, the Privilege Camp for which prisoners paid for better accommodation and food and also a Jewish Camp where the inmates were provided with kosher food. It seems that the camp closed by late March or early April 1919. For the most part three marks were applied to mail, namely two types of double oval cachets and the single circle PC although a small number of other cachets have been found used at this camp. Censor labels were also used if required. The colours used for the marks are blue, purple, violet, red or pink which could be applied both on dispatch or receipt but not with any consistency, some mail existing with no camp markings. Postings which exceeded the permitted number of letters for free postage incurred normal postal rates if allowed.

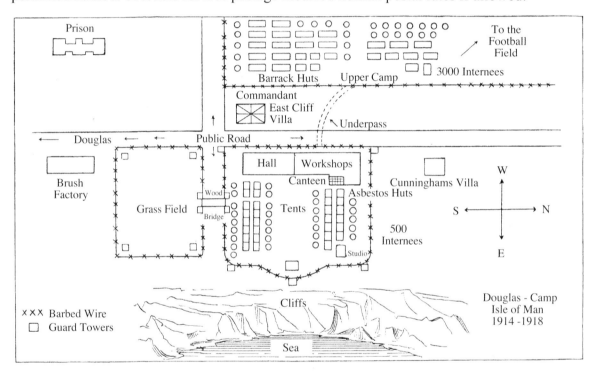

Sketch map of Douglas Camp based on F.L.Dunbar-Kaldreuth's, "Die Männerinsel".

120	1914	ALIENS' CAMP / CENSORED/. *ISLE OF MAN * small d/o	Red/violet	G
121	1915	ALIENS' DETENTION CAMP /CENSORED/ + DOUGLAS, I.O.M. + d/o	Red/ blue Pink/violet	F
122	1919	ALIENS' CAMP / DOUGLAS/ * LABOUR DEPARTMENT * d/o	Red	G
123	1916	"JEWISH COMMITTEE" s/l Internee produced?	Red	G
124	1917	PRISONER OF WAR s/l Possibly applied in transit from London.	Blue	G
125	1917	Verein für / Leicht-Athletik / Douglas Lager, I.o.M. Triangular h/s encloses 3 legs, internee produced?	Blue-green	G
126	1917	Cover from Douglas Camp with 43mm s/l BUSINESS LETTER	Black	G

127	1919	LT-COL.,COMMANDANT, ALIENS' CAMP, DOUGLAS d/l	Violet	H
128	1914-19	Registered ps cover from Douglas Camp canc. Douglas s/o or s/c	N/A	K
129	1914-19	Envelope printed DOUGLAS ALIENS CAMP/ ISLE OF MAN	Black	G
130	1914-19	Letter-sheet printed DOUGLAS ALIENS CAMP/ ISLE OF MAN	Black	B
131	1914-19	Postcards - internee designed Values depend on scarcity	N/A	F - H
132	1914-19	Postcards, photographic, often by W.H. Warburton or D. Collister & Son, both of Douglas	B/ W	F - H

120

121

122

"JEWISH COMMITTEE"

123

PRISONER OF WAR.

124

BUSINESS LETTER.

126

125

127

Douglas Aliens' Camp,

Isle of Man,

.........................191

REGULATION LETTER.

Letters written in English will
have Priority.

130

128

Christmas postcard designed by Douglas Internee G. A. Bredow in 1916 (131).

Christmas postcard hand drawn by Douglas Internee in 1914 (131).

Photographic postcard of Douglas Internee Athletic Group in 1915 (132).

Plate 1. This photographic postcard, by D. Collister & Son, Douglas, posted on 25th July 1914 shows Cunningham Camp as it was just before the outbreak of war. Already capable of taking a large number of young men on holiday, it is clear why the authorities thought it an ideal location for Internees to be interned.

Plate 2. The men interned in Douglas Camp had a wide range of activities to occupy their time. This postcard, by W. H. Warburton, Douglas, of the workshop shows a selection of items that were produced, the conditions in which they were made and the men who worked there.

DOUGLAS I.O.M., CUNNINGHAMS' HOLIDAY CAMP   401.

Plate 3: The Douglas Prisoner of War Camp was based in the former holiday establishment for young men known as "Cunningham's Camp". The postcard shown here from the Manx Art Series was probably taken soon after the cessation of hostilities in November 1918 and the closure of the camp in June 1919. It shows the tents which were such a feature of the WW1 accommodation as well as the more permanent buildings which were erected during the war and were used for many years after the war when the camp returned to its function as a holiday venue.

Plate 4. Guard Sergeants outside Falcon Cliff in WW I.

Plan of Knockaloe Camp

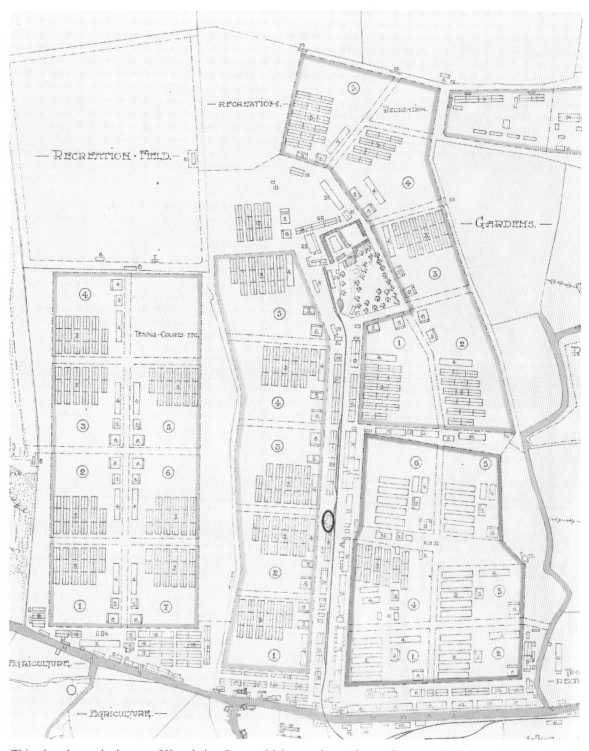

This plan shows the layout of Knockaloe Camp which was almost three miles around with nearly 700 miles of barbed wire used in the fences and 70 miles of electric cable provided power for over 7100 lights.

"By permission of Manx National Heritage MNH-p.2024"

Key

Camp 1	Pink		Railway	Black
Camp 2	Yellow		Roads	Orange
Camp 3	Violet		Farm	Black
Camp 4	Blue-green		Post Office	Red circle
Guards Camp	Brown			

Knockaloe

This camp was based at Knockaloe Farm, and from November 1914 began accommodating internees. Douglas Camp which came into use on 22nd September 1914 was rapidly filled and by October 1914 was full. After an inspection of various sites by British officials Knockaloe was deemed the best venue to house a new camp. The area had been used for several years as a camp for Territorial Force and Volunteer Battalions and the advantages of the site were considered good, namely sheltered from prevailing wind by surrounding hills and well drained. It was situated only a few miles from Peel and a short railway line came from that city to the camp to transport the enormous quantities of materials and supplies needed for an establishment which reached a population of near 23,000 souls. For such a large population it is surprising that philatelic items from the camp are relatively scarce but perhaps less so than material from Douglas Camp. The camp closed well after the armistice on 11th November 1918 and was not cleared until late summer 1919. In October 1919 the sale of the site and contents took place.

For the most part three types of marks were applied to mail, namely two types of double oval cachets and the single circle PC. However since the publication of the catalogues of Whitney and Field a number of varieties have been noted and are for the first time identified in this publication though the list is representative rather than definitive and further variants are likely to be recorded. As in Douglas Camp censor labels were also used if required. The colours usually used for the marks are blue, violet, red or pink which could be applied both on dispatch or receipt but not with any consistency with some mail existing with no camp markings. Postings which exceeded the permitted number of letters for free postage incurred normal postal rates if allowed. The camp had its own sub post office from 1915 with a dedicated double circle hand stamp and registered labels. Various other types of cachet, some of which are previously unrecorded, are also listed together with various postal stationery items.

140	1914	ALIENS' DETENTION CAMP / CENSORED/ *KNOCKALOE, I.O.M. * d/o Maltese cross stars	Black/violet blue	E
141	1917	As above but with 3 broken horizontal lines x 2 d/o Maltese cross stars	Violet	F
142	1915	As above but four dots replace Maltese cross and two horizontal lines, d/o	Violet	F
143	1916	As above but a + replaces Maltese cross d/o, also seen with no "O" in I.O.M.	Violet	F
144	1916	As above but one upper single line with broken top, with crosses, d/o	Violet/blue	F
145	1917	As above but upper & lower lines in two parts d/o left cross absent	Violet	F
146	1916	ALIENS' DETENTION CAMP / CENSORED/ KNOCKALOE, I.O.M., d/o dots replace stars with two horizontal daggers	Violet	F
147	1918	As above but horizontal daggers split in two	Violet/black	F

148	1914	KNOCKALOE ALIENS' CAMP +ISLE OF MAN + small t/ o + cross stars 40 x 27mm	Violet/blue	G
149	1916	As above but no crosses stars (also seen with only left star)	Violet	G
150	1917	+GARRISON OFFICE+ / ROYAL DEFENCE CORPS/ No.___ / KNOCKALOE CAMP, ISLE OF MAN dated d/o	Red/blue	H
150a	1915-19	INDUSTRIAL DEPARTMENT/ CAMP III KNOCKALOE / ISLE OF MAN, Undated d/o	Blue	F
151	1915	THE CAMP. KNOCKALOE/ PEEL Timed & dated d/c short medium arcs	Black	F
152	1915	Knockaloe registered cover with Peel label with PEEL s/c CDS	Black	J
153	1915	As 151 used registered with general purpose label or Knockaloe label 153a (see also 114)	Black	K
154	1915	Loose labels	Black	D
155	1915	Lieut. Colonel/ Commandant/ Knockaloe Aliens' Camp 3/L cachet	Blue	F
156	1918	SUB-COMMANDANT/ No. 1 CAMP small 2/L cachet	Black	F
157	1916	............./ ASSISTANT COMMANDANT/ FOR COMMANDANT 3/L cachet	Violet	F
158	1915?	Hospital s/L cachet hand cut	Purple	I
159	1916	KNOCKALOE CAMP/ PEEL I.O.M. 2/L cachet Used as transit mark ex Germany forwarded to U.K.	Purple	I
160	1916?	Knockaloe stamp perf. 11 hand cut unofficial h/s Internee produced. Scarce (Beware of forgeries)	Rose	P
160a	1916?	Stamp on cover cancelled with a hand-cut cachet	Black	P
161	1914-19	Envelope printed ALIENS' DETENTION CAMP/ KNOCKALOE,/ ISLE OF MAN ps used.	Black	F
162	1917	Envelope printed Prisoners' Aid Society,/ Camp 1/ Knockaloe, Isle of Man. ps used.	Black	G
163	1917	Envelope printed Markel Committee/ Camp 1/ Knockaloe, I.O.M. ps used.	Black	G

164	1914-19	Letter-sheet printed KNOCKALOE ALIENS CAMP/ ISLE OF MAN on Regulation Letter, ps	Black	D
165	1915	Wrapper "KNOCKALOE LAGER ZEITUNG" Printed for newspapers ps	Black	E
165a	1915	Wrapper "KNOCKALOE LAGER ECHO" Printed for newspapers ps	Black	E
166	1914?	Label PAID LETTERS / For Prisoner of War Camp/ ISLE OF MAN. Adhesive 113mm x 73mm on pale blue paper	Black	F
167	1914?	Printed Label 152mm x 90mm G/L Mr........../Knockaloe Camp, Peel, I.o.M./ Registered Number....../ Camp Number...../ Compound Number...........	Black	D
168	1914-19	Postcards internee designed Values depend on scarcity.	N/A	G
169	1914-19	Postcards photographic Values depend on scarcity.	N/A	H

Seen above is the unauthorised Knockaloe rose coloured stamp on an internally used cover with an internee produced hand cut single ring handstamp, from the Mannin Collections Archive with permission (160a).

140

141

142

143

144

145

146

147

148

149

150

150a

151

152

153

153a

154

155

156

ASSISTANT COMMANDANT
FOR COMMANDANT

157

158

KNOCKALOE CAMP
PEEL   I.O.M.

159

160

ALIENS' DETENTION CAMP,
KNOCKALOE,
ISLE OF MAN.

161

Prisoners' Aid Society,
Camp I,
Knockaloe, Isle of Man.

162

Markel Committee
Camp I.
Kaockaloe I. O. M.

163

REGULATION LETTER.

Letters written in English will
have Priority.

Knockaloe Aliens' Camp,
Isle of Man.

164

Evidence that Postage Due stamps were applied at the Knockaloe Post Office between 1917 and 1919 is indicated by the use of the double circle date stamp THE CAMP KNOCKALOE / PEEL cancelling the stamp(s) shown here enlarged.

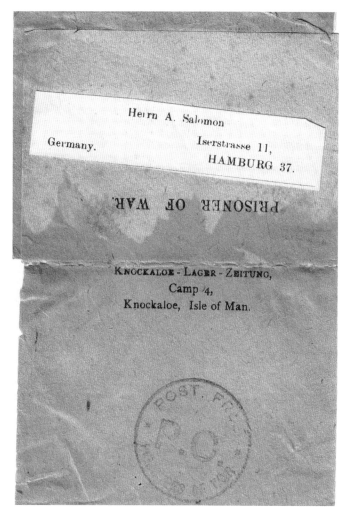

165

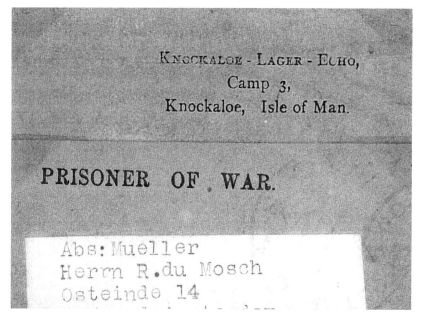

165a

PAID LETTERS

FOR

Prisoner of War Camp

ISLE OF MAN

DATE STAMP

Bundle made up by _____

This label should accompany any report in respect of correspondence received in this bundle.

Cette étiquette doit accompagner toute plainte à l'égard des correspondances reçues dans cette liasse.

166

Mr. *H. C. Martens.*

Knockaloe Camp,

Peel, I.o.M.

Great Britain.

Registered Number *4062*

Camp Number *I*

Compound Number *V Hut 4B.*

167: Postal Stationery printed label.

168: Knockaloe Postcard designed by internee G. Stolz dated 1917.

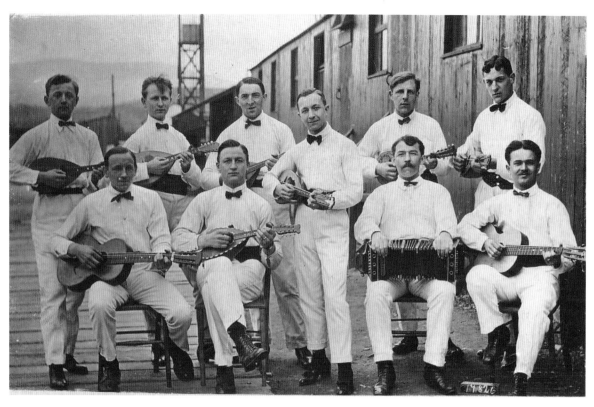

169: Knockaloe photographic Postcard by D. W. Kees, Shore Road, Peel.

169: Seen above is a photographic postcard of an orchestra made up of Prisoners of War seated in front of huts in Knockaloe Camp. Concerts were a regular feature of camp life by this and other musical groups. In her book "Hedge of Thorns" about the life of Voirrey Kelly as a child living in the village of Patrick alongside the camp, Pat Kelly records her memories of the delightful sounds coming from the camp at night:

*"When the music, the songs and the laughter began. Voirrey opened the window to allow it unbridled entry ...
every shadow in the room rose and danced to the music".*

WW1 Transit Marks

Many covers to and from internment camps in the Isle of Man bear marks applied by censors and postal authorities as they travelled between their destinations. As is often the case almost every item will attract a differing range of marks and those listed here cannot be regarded as definitive. However those shown give an idea of some of the marks encountered in the compilation of this catalogue and give an idea of the range of marks which were used both in transit, on receipt or on redirection. The values are for marks without other camp cachets on plain covers or tuck-ins. If found with other marks of higher value, the higher values take precedence. Dates given are those of items seen and earlier or later dates of use may exist.

170	1915	-NO CHARGE FOR POSTAGE-/ -PRISONER OF WAR MAIL- NEW YORK, N.Y.- 3/L h/s applied New York on cvr ex IOM	Black	E
171	1917	No charge for postage Prisoner / of War Mail New York N.Y. 2/L h/s	Violet / red / black	E
172	1918	ENGLISH CORRESPONDENCE /REGD/No Dated d/o applied London ex Knockaloe	Violet / blue-black	D
173	1916	PRISONERS OF WAR / *INFORMATION BUREAU* t/o with crown	Violet	D
174	1916	ZENSUR / ARTEILUNG/ WIEN Triangular box applied Vienna ex Knockaloe	Red	D
175	1915	Zurück dated double bx h/s Knockaloe – Germany	Violet	D
176	1919	REPATRIATED s/l h/s 38mm s/l Chemnitz-Dgls	Grey	F
177	1915	Prisonnier de guerre bx h/s on cvr Germany - Douglas	Purple	F
178	1915?	Ubgereift / parti box paper label Douglas - Hamburg	Green / black	C
179	1915	Unbefannt / incunnu box paper label Knockaloe-Germany	Green / black	C
180	1916	Schriftleitung der/Knockaloe Lagerzeitung,/ fruher "Stobsiade,"/ Internment Camp, Knockaloe/ Camp 4 Compound 1. 5 line cachet on cvr - Berlin	Violet / blue	E
181	1919	Repatrie / RETOUR bx h/s	Black	F
182	1915	Released from internment /RETURN TO SENDER/ PRISONERS OF WAR / INFORMATION BUREAU	Green	F
183	1916	Auslandstelle Emmerich */ Frei-gegeben d/c used Germany-IOM both directions	Violet	D
184	1916	ÜBERNACHUNGOSTELLE/*METZ* Geprüft und Frei-gegeben d/c Germany-Douglas	Blue	D

NO CHARGE FOR POSTAGE
PRISONER OF WAR MAIL
NEW YORK, N.Y.

170

No charge for postage Prisoner
of War Mail New York, N. Y.

171

ENGLISH CORRESPONDENCE
REGd 1 8 SEP. 1918
No.

172

PRISONERS OF WAR
INFORMATION BUREAU

173

ZENSUR-ABTEILUNG WIEN

174

Zurück
24 APR 1915

175

REPATRIATED.

176

Prisonnier de guerre

177

Abgereist,
ohne Angabe der Adresse.
parti,
sans laisser d'adresse.

178

Unbekannt.
inconnu.

179

Schriftleitung der
Knockaloe Lagerzeitung,
früher "Stobsiade."
Internment Camp, Knockaloe
Camp 4   Compound 1

180

P. W. I. B.
Repatrie
RETOUR
Return to Sender

181

Auslandstelle Emmerich
Frei-gegeben

183

Released from internment.
RETURN TO SENDER.
Der Kriegsgefangene ist entlassen
PRISONERS OF WAR
INFORMATION BUREAU

182

ÜBERNACHUNGSSTELLE
Geprüft
und frei-gegeben
METZ

184

185

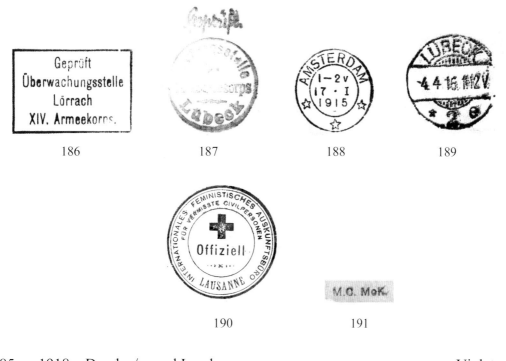

186   187   188   189

190   191

185	1918	Dumb s/c used London	Violet	C
186	1914?	Geprüft / Überwachungsstelle / Lörrach / XIV. Armeekorps boxed	Purple	E
187	1916	Geprüft s/l XI Aribuescorps / Lübeck s/c on Feldpost Germany-Douglas	Violet	E
188	1916	AMSTERDAM 3*dated d/c type used as receiver or dispatch CDS	Black	C
189	1916	LUBECK dated "Bridge" type h/s used as receiver or dispatch CDS**	Black	C
190	1918	Offiziell Lausanne Red Cross triple circle 39mm various styles	Blue/black	F
191	1914-19	Censor initials in small hand stamp on mail to foreign countries. This is 14mm x 2mm. Seven types known so far – E.B., D.S.C, G.E.F. (boxed), M.C.McK, O.McK, E.C.M, and H.G.M	Violet/pink /black	F

** N.B. This is an example of a "Bridge" hand stamp of which there are many hundreds. For detailed information a relevant specialised catalogue should be referred to such as the Michel catalogue.

Two examples of transit marks including IOMPHS 173 on the upper one used on a postal stationery cover from Douglas to London the lower item showing the previously unrecorded "Return to sender" cachet, IOMPHS 182, used on an incoming registered cover from Amsterdam to Knockaloe as the recipient, on parole, was not at the camp. Such items illustrate how a range of marks may be found adding considerable interest to postal historians.

Shown here is an example of various marks in use on a Feldpost item from Lübeck to Knockaloe.

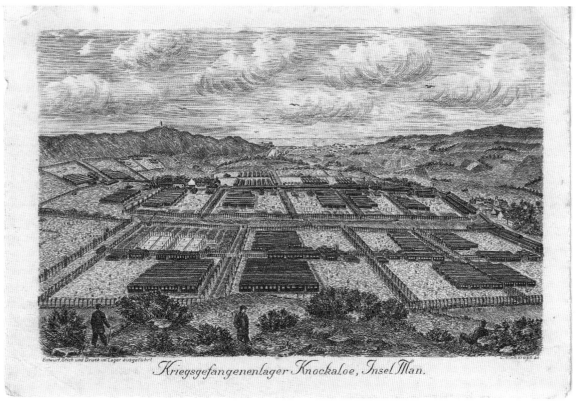

An etching of Knockaloe camp, of post card size, designed by C. Schneider & printed on card in the camp.

The Second World War

Introduction

During the Second World War there were plans to send enemy aliens to the British Dominions. However partly due to the loss of life after the sinking of the liner Arandora Star en route to Newfoundland carrying Italians and Germans the authorities decided to use facilities based in the British Isles. One result was that camps were opened in Douglas, Onchan, Ramsey, Peel and a large area of the south of the Isle of Man centred around Port Erin and Port St Mary. For the most part these camps made use of existing establishments used in peacetime for tourist accommodation, though some private houses may have been included. The owners usually had to move from their homes to make way for the incoming internees taking a few personal items.

Early on in the war Enemy Alien Tribunals were set up to classify both men and women aliens into one of three categories. Category A aliens posed a potential threat and were to be interned at once. Category B aliens were those whose loyalty was a little suspect but who could remain at liberty and category C people who posed no risk. Once on the Island it was not long before several internees were released after they had satisfied certain conditions, for example if they were prepared to use skills which they had to assist the war effort. Strict rules were imposed as to where such persons could live. As a result of this some camps were short lived and in the case of the Regent (located in Regent Street/Loch Promenade) never used for internees. Others were transferred for other uses as required, namely Central and Granville. The Sefton was returned to the owners in May 1941.

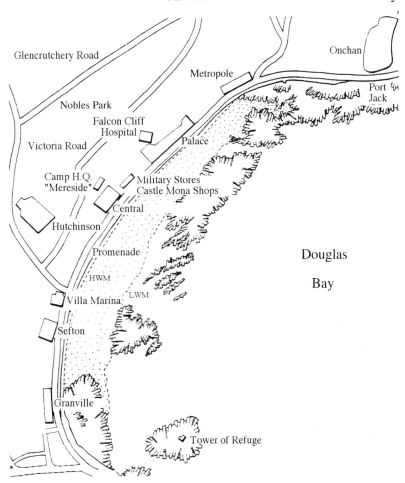

A map showing the location of the Douglas based Internment Camps during the Second World War.

Unlike the previous war the Cunningham Holiday Camp was not used for internees but was commissioned as billeting for the H.M.S. St George training establishment in September 1939. The boy trainees housed there went to the newly built Ballakermeen School for classes. The Howstrake Holiday Camp near Groudle Glen was used for the Junior Section of the Royal Navy School of Music from July 1941 until July 1946. It may be that this camp had been considered for use to house internees but in fact this did not happen.

Extract from Home Office Orders for Internment Camps

These orders were dated 30th June 1943 and were stated to include all amendments. They are of great interest in particular giving the letter codes for each camp.

CORRESPONDENCE

101. The Commandant will keep posted in the Camp the following Standing Orders for Internees (correspondence):-

A. Letters from internees must be written in ink, distinctly, in plain language of which the meaning is clear. Alien internees should write in their own language rather than faulty English. If any other language than English, German or Italian is used, the writer must indicate on the outside of the letter when folded the language in which it is written (e.g., "Letter in Czech").

Internees should warn their correspondents who write to them from any address in the British Isles that their letters may be stopped by the censor unless they contain the full postal address of the writer. Letters without such, or signed with initials or forenames only, will not be delivered.

To avoid delay and to assist the postal authority, letters have been allotted to civilian internment in the Isle of Man as follows:-

Ballaquane Hospital	*ZR*
Falcon Cliff Hospital	*ZM*
Hutchinson (Germans)	*P*
Hutchinson (Hungarians)	*PH*
Hutchinson (Japanese)	*PJ*
Hutchinson (Rumanians)	*PR*
Mooragh (Finns)	*F*
Mooragh (Germans)	*L*
Mooragh (Italians)	*N*
Metropole	*S*
Onchan	*O*
Peel* (British detainees)	*M*
Peel* (Alien detainees)	*X*
Port Erin* (Women)	*W*
Port Erin* (Married couples)	*Y*

(*N.B. Peel may be referred to as "Peveril" and Port Erin as "Rushen")

Internees should warn their correspondents to address correspondence accordingly. Any letters incorrectly addressed will be delayed in delivery.

B. Two letters only may be written weekly, and must be confined to private affairs and to business matters in which the writer has a personal interest. Letters must be written on the official note paper provided unless addressed to British Government Departments, Public Offices, any Court of Justice, or Advisory Committees. Correspondence with the press is prohibited. Without special permission from the

Commandant, these two letters will not be dispatched on the same day. The privilege of writing two letters a week may not be transferred to another internee ("Borrowed Letters"). No internee may use one of his two letters to write on behalf of another internee. A letter must be written with the lines running across the breadth of the paper and not lengthways. A letter must not contain more than 24 lines without permission of the Commandant, and such permission to write an extra letter, will normally only be granted if the internee has affairs of special importance to discuss in connection with his business, detention or emigration. If permission is granted, the letter should be handed in separately from the remainder of the internee mail, in order to avoid interception by the Censor for contravention of the rules.

C. No letter may contain a cypher, code, musical notation or symbols, sketch, unintelligible mark or sign, shorthand symbol, quotation from or to a reference book or any objectionable matter. Manuscript musical score sheets will not be permitted.

D. Letters must give the full name and address of the addressee. Initials only are not admissible, nor may letters be sent care of a post office or to an accommodation address, or to a third party for re-direction.

E. If an internee wishes to send enclosures with his letters or to register a letter, he should apply to the Commandant for the permission for the letter to be sent in an envelope. In the case of a letter to be registered the postage must be paid in advance.

The following letters should be handed in separately from the ordinary internee mail, and should not be stuck down:-

a) Letters to British Government Departments, Public Offices or any Advisory Committee to which he is entitled to make representations.
b) Letter to a Foreign Embassy, Legation or Consulate.
c) Special letters of an urgent character to solicitors.
d) Letters to any Court of Justice.

Any other letters may be stuck down by adhesive label only.

F. Letters by Prisoners of War mail from German and Italian internees to Germany and Italy respectively are sent by air all the way without charge. In all other cases, air mail outward is not allowed without the permission of the Commandant and, when granted, postage must be prepaid by the internee.

Douglas: Official Paid

201	1940	OFFICIAL PAID dated s/c 24mm	Red	C
202	1940	OFFICIAL PAID dated s/c 30mm	Red	C
203	1940	OPENED BY / EXAMINER various numbers Printed label, usually on private or tuck in items	Black	C
203a	1940	OPENED BY / CENSOR various numbers Printed label, usually on private or tuck in items	Black	C
204	1940	NO TRACE ISLE OF MAN s/l	Violet	F
204a	1940	RETURN TO SENDER s/l	Violet	G

NO TRACE, ISLE OF MAN

204

RETURN TO SENDER

204a

201   202   204a

P.C. 90

OPENED BY

EXAMINER 3687

51—851—W.H.H. Ltd.

P.C. 66

OPENED BY

CENSOR

1006

203   203a

Douglas: Headquarters Post Office

The Headquarters Post Office dealt with mail in and out of Isle of Man internment camps as well as returning mail addressed to persons of whom there was no trace on the Island or had been released. Not all internee mail received Headquarters cachets.

205	1945	HEADQUARTERS / ISLE OF MAN GARRISON dated t/o	Violet/black	G
206	1940	CAMP s/l	Black	H
207	1940	HEADQUARTERS POST OFFICE / INTERN CAMPS, DOUGLAS, I.O.M. dated t/o	Violet/blue	F
208	1941	HEADQUARTERS INTERNMENT CAMPS / DOUGLAS, ISLE OF MAN dated t/o	Red/violet	G
209	1942	HEADQUARTERS POST OFFICE / INTERN. CAMPS, DOUGLAS, I.O.M. dated d/o	Violet	F
210	1941	Hd. QRS /POST OFFICE/DOUGLAS .I.O.M. dated lg s/c	Violet/black	H
211	1940	RELEASED HEADQUARTERS POST OFFICE/ INT. CAMPS./ I.O.M. dated lg s/c	Violet	I
212	1940	NO TRACE / H.Q. I.O.M. d/l	Violet	G

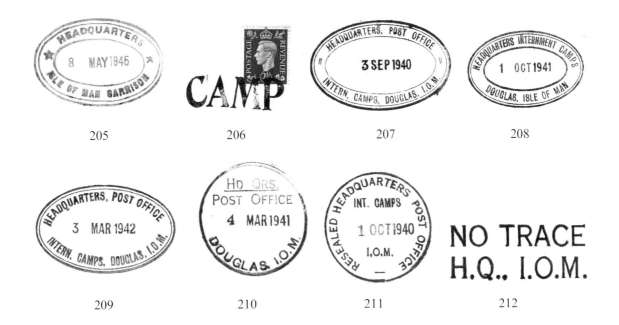

| 205 | 206 | 207 | 208 |

| 209 | 210 | 211 | 212 |

Douglas: Central Camp

This camp was used for only a short time. It was opened on 13th June 1940 and closed during April 1941 when it was taken over as a Ground Defence Gunnery School. Situated on Central Promenade, Castle Drive, Mona Drive and Empress Drive, Douglas, the camp made used of some forty boarding houses or hotels. It is thought to have housed some 2000 German internees.

213	1940	CENTRAL-CAMP-DOUGLAS / POST-POST s/c hand cut	Red or Black	H
214	1940	CENTRAL INTERNMENT CAMP / DOUGLAS / I.O.M. d/o	Black	F
215	1940	CENTRAL INTERNMENT CAMP / No. / DOUGLAS / I.O.M. dated d/o	Violet	F
216	1940	OFFICER I/C WELFARE ORGANISATION/ PROMENADE, CENTRAL CAMP DOUGLAS, I.O.M. t/o	Violet	H
217	1940	CENTRAL INTERNMENT CAMP / POST OFFICE bx	Red	H
218	1940	PASSED BY CENSOR / No. / CENTRAL INTERNMENT CAMP / DOUGLAS, I.O.M. ..../CAPT unframed	Violet	G
219	1940	PLEASE RE-DIRECT TO/..../.... bx	Red	G
220	1940	TRANSFERRED TO /....... CAMP bx	Red	G
221	1940	NOT CENTRAL s/o	Black	H

222	1940	CENTRAL / INTERNMENT CAMP/ DOUGLAS, I.O.M./REC'D bx dated	Violet	H
223	1940	RELEASED	Violet	H

213

214

215

216

CENTRAL INTERNMENT CAMP
POST OFFICE.

217

PASSED BY CENSOR
No.
CENTRAL INTERNMENT CAMP
DOUGLAS, I.O.M.

.... CAPT,

218

PLEASE RE-DIRECT TO

219

TRANSFERRED TO

.... CAMP

220

NOT CENTRAL

221

CENTRAL
INTERNMENT CAMP.
DOUGLAS, I.O.M.
REC'D. 12 SEP 1940

222

RELEASED

223

CLOCKTOWER & PROMENADE. DOUGLAS. I.O.M.

Plate 5: A photographic postcard of the Loch Promenade prior to WW II. The Granville Camp comprised the group of buildings to the right and left of the church in the centre.

Plate 6: A photograph of Falcon Cliff in 2014. This building was used as a military hospital in WW II and is largely unchanged from that era.

Douglas: Falcon Cliff Hospital (ZM Camp)

Falcon Cliff Hospital, with 65 to 80 beds, was situated in the former Falcon Cliff Hotel on Palace Road on the high ground behind Douglas Promenade. For the most part it housed short term male internees, with acute cases being sent to Noble's Hospital in Douglas, the main civilian facility of the Island.

225	1941	FALCON CLIFF HOSPITAL/ ISLE OF MAN dated d/o	Violet	G
226	1941	FALCON CLIFF HOSPITAL/ ISLE OF MAN small OF, dated d/o	Violet	G
227	1945	Z M CAMP / ISLE OF MAN small OF, dated d/o	Black	G
228	1941	SPECIAL PERMISSION box. hex. (No examples found to date)	Violet?	G

225   226   227

Douglas: Granville (T Camp)

This camp, based on a group of boarding houses adjoining and including the Granville Hotel on Loch Promenade, was used mainly for Italian internees from October 1940 to October 1941. It then became part of H.M.S. VALKYRIE, a radar training facility for the Royal Navy.

230	1940	GRANVILLE INTERNMENT CAMP / DOUGLAS, I.O.M. dated d/o	Violet	G
231	1940	GRANVILLE INTERNMENT CAMP / No. / DOUGLAS, I.O.M. dated d/o	Red	G

230   231

Douglas: Hutchinson (P Camp)

This camp was situated on Hutchinson Square in Douglas using all the houses both for the accommodation and administration of German and Austrian internees. It was opened in mid July 1940 and closed as P Camp during March 1944. In Home Office Orders for internment Camps, published 1943, camp codes were given for other nationalities, Hungarians PH, Japanese PJ and Romanians PR, however to date items bearing these codes have not been seen. It may be that at a local level all mail received the code P whatever the nationality of the sender. After closure any remaining internees were transferred to Peveril camp in Peel. In November 1944 German Prisoners of War were located in these houses which became part of 171 POW Camp. It finally closed on August 4th 1945 and was returned to the owners in November of the same year.

235	1940	HUTCHINSON INTERNMENT CAMP / No. / DOUGLAS. / I.O.M. dated d/o	Black / Violet	F
236	1941	"P" CAMP / ISLE OF MAN dated d/o	Red / Green	H
237	1942	"P" CAMP / No. ISLE OF MAN dated d/o	Purple	H
238	1944	SPECIAL PERMISSION bx hex	Green, Violet, Red	I
239	1940	NOT HUTCHINSON CAMP / DOUGLAS. 2/ L unframed	Violet	G
240	1941	HUTCHINSON s/l unframed	Blue	F
241	1942	HUTCHINSON / CAMP dated d/c	Violet	F
242	1940	Postal stationery printed card no camp address	Black on buff	G
242a	1940	Postal stationery printed card with camp address HUTCHINSON INTERNMENT CAMP/ DOUGLAS, / I.O.M.	Black on buff	G
243	1944	Postal stationery printed card camp address HUTCHINSON INTERNMENT CAMP, / DOUGLAS / ISLE OF MAN. ..../ Major / Camp Commander	Black on white	G
244	1940	Internee photo hand drawn or duplicated Postcard	N/A	G
244a	1940	Photographic postcard	N/A	G

235

236

237

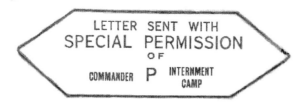

238

NOT HUTCHINSON CAMP.
DOUGLAS.

239

HUTCHINSON

240

241

NOTHING is to be written on this side except the date, signature and address of the sender. Erase words not required. **IF ANYTHING ELSE IS ADDED THE POSTCARD WILL BE DESTROYED.**

I am (not) well.

I have been admitted into Hospital {sick / for operation} and am going on well.

I am being transferred to another camp.

I have received your card dated ....

Signature. HERBERT HIRSCHMANN

Camp Address..............................

Date ....

(1007) Demand 7673 250m (9) 7/40 **Gp.697** C&SLtd

242

NOTHING to be written on this side except the date, signature and address of the sender. Erase words not required. **IF ANYTHING ELSE IS ADDED THE POSTCARD WILL BE DESTROYED.**

I am (not) well.

I have been admitted into Hospital {sick / for operation} and am going on well.

I am being transferred to another camp.

I have received your card dated ....

Signature ..... *Heinrich Hirsch* .....

HUTCHINSON INTERNMENT CAMP
DOUGLAS, I.o.M.

House 41.

Date ..... 14. 8. 1940 .....

Wt. P.4444—1250/7/40. N.M.P., Ltd.

242a

es/1.33

HUTCHINSON INTERNMENT CAMP,
DOUGLAS,
ISLE OF MAN.

24th January 1944

E.T.C. Ötvös

Your communication of *21st January 1944*
duly received, ~~enclosing~~ *Treasury notes £5:0:0d.*

for Major,
Camp Commander.

Wt.P. 8646. 1000/12/42, W. Newby & Sons.

243

244

244a: Private collection with permission.

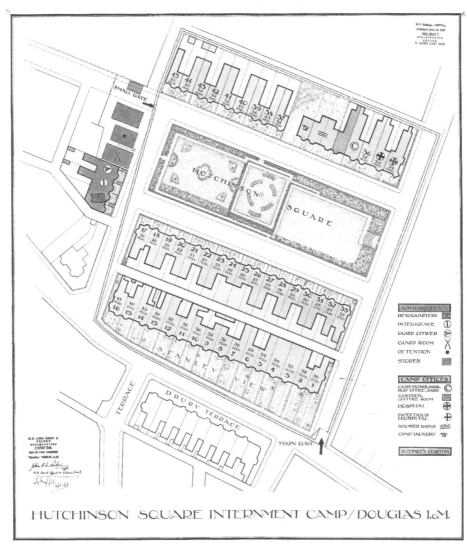

Plate 7: A map of Hutchinson Camp, with permission Manx National Heritage.

Plate 8: Roll call at Hutchinson Camp. Private collection with permission.

Plate 9: Hutchinson Camp looking towards the sea. Private collection with permission.

Plate 10: Administration Block and Store Huts outside wire of Hutchinson Camp.
View from roof in North-West corner looking towards South-West. Private collection with permission.

Douglas: Metropole (S Camp)

This camp, based on a group of boarding houses adjoining and including the Metropole Hotel on Queen's Promenade, Douglas was used mainly for Italian internees with some Germans from July 1940 to November 1944. It then became part of 171 P.O.W. Camp until early March 1945.

245	1940	METROPOLE INTERNMENT CAMP / No. / DOUGLAS, I.O.M. dated d/o	Black/violet	G
246	1940	METROPOLE INTERNMENT CAMP / No. / DOUGLAS, I.O.M. undated d/o	Violet/purple	G
247	1941	"S"CAMP / No. / DOUGLAS, I.(O.M.?) dated d/o	Violet	G
248	1943	LETTER SENT WITH / SPECIAL PERMISSION / OF / COMMANDER S INTERNMENT / CAMP bx .hex.	Violet	I

245

246

247

248

Douglas: Onchan (O Camp)

This camp, based on a group of boarding houses on Royal Avenue, Onchan and others overlooking Douglas Bay, was used from June 1940 mainly for Germans and Austrians, many, according to Whitney, were merchants and civilians from Manchester. These then during July 1941 were transferred to Hutchinson Camp. From September 1941 the camp was used for Italian internees. The camp closed in November 1944 to alien internees and became part of P.O.W. Camp 171 in early March 1945. The final closure date is uncertain but was probably soon after May 1945.

250	1940	ONCHAN INTERNMENT CAMP bx s/l	Red	G
251	1940	ONCHAN INTERNMENT CAMP unboxed s/l Thin letters	Black/violet	F
252	1940	ONCHAN INTERNMENT CAMP unboxed s/l Round letters	Blue	F
253	1940	O INTERNMENT CAMP unboxed s/l Thin letters (251 cut down)	Black/violet	G
254	1940	ONCHAN INTERNMENT CAMP/ CAMP POST OFFICE dated d/o	Black/violet red or blue	F
255	1940	ONCHAN INTERNMENT CAMP/ No. / ONCHAN, I.O.M. dated d/o	Black/violet	G
256	1940	O, CAMP POST OFFICE/ ONCHAN, I.O.M. dated d/o	Black/violet	G
257	1941	O INTERNMENT CAMP / POST OFFICE / I.O.M. dated d/o "O" in m/s	Violet	G
258	1941	OFFICER i/c WELFARE ORGANISATION / ONCHAN CAMP / ONCHAN, I.O.M. m/s dated t/o	Violet	I
259	1942	LETTER SENT WITH / SPECIAL PERMISSION / OF / COMMANDER S INTERNMENT / CAMP, bx .hex.	Violet	I
260	1941	NOT AT ONCHAN-PLEASE FORWARD TO / bx duplicated label	Black	H/I
261	1942	ONCHAN / CAMP dated d/c	Red	H
262	1940	Internee drawn or duplicated postcard	N/A	H/I
262a	1940	Photographic postcard	N/A	G
263	1940	Credited on / Your Account / RECEIPT incl. 3/l 80mm x 26mm used with / PAY DAYS / TUESD. OR THURS. 2/l, 60mm x 10mm, used on Reg. Cover.	Blue	H
264	1940	ONCHAN INTERNMENT CAMP / INTERNEES OFFICE dated d/o.	Blue	G/H

250

251

252

253

254

255

256

257

258

259

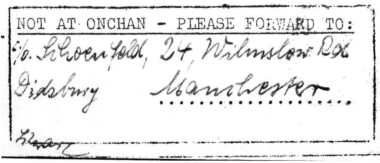

260

261

264

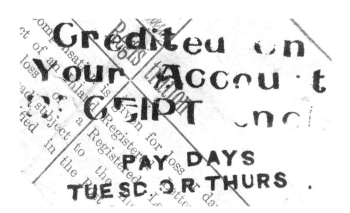

263

262a: The gate at Onchan Camp.

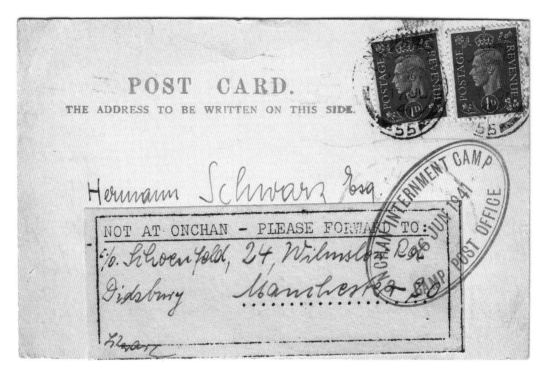

Two items from Onchan Camp including on the upper one the previously unrecorded "Not at Onchan-Please Forward to" duplicated label, IOMPHS 260, used together with the double oval Onchan Internment Camp cachet, IOMPHS 254, on a postcard redirected from Douglas to Manchester, the lower one a duplicated "Greetings" postcard, IOMPHS type 262, by an internee showing Father Christmas with gun and gifts in Onchan Camp and dated 1941.

Douglas: Palace (R Camp)

This camp was based on a group of twenty eight boarding houses on Palace Terrace and four on Palace View. It was used mainly for Italian internees from 22nd June 1940 to November 1941. The road and land adjoining these properties was closed to the public soon after 2nd July 1940 by the erection of barbed wire. During November 1941 the camp closed for a short time, the existing internees being moved on. The camp came into use again during December 1941 when Japanese, Hungarian, Finnish and Romanian internees were housed. Palace Camp finally closed during November 1942 when any remaining inmates were transferred to Mooragh Camp, Ramsey. In January 1943 it is thought that the camp was then used to house the First Company of the Special Operations Training Battalion.

265	1940	PALACE INTERNMENT CAMP/ DOUGLAS s/c	Violet/black	F
266	1940	PALACE INTERNMENT CAMP / No. / DOUGLAS, I.O.M. d/o	Violet	F
267	1941	PALACE INTERNMENT CAMP / POST OFFICE / DOUGLAS, I.O.M. d/o	Violet/black	F
268	1941	R INTERNMENT CAMP / POST OFFICE/ DOUGLAS, I.O.M. dated d/o m/s R	Violet	G
268a	1941	R INTERNMENT CAMP / POST OFFICE/ I.O.M. dated d/o m/s R, Douglas deleted.	Violet	G
269	1942	INTELLIGENCE OFFICER/ "R" CAMP, DOUGLAS dated d/o	Violet	K
270	1942	SPECIAL LETTER / R CAMP / AUTHORISED BY COMMANDER double box hex.	Violet	I

265

266

267

268

268a

269

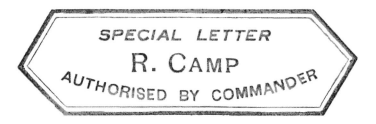

270

Plate 11: Palace Terrace with armed guard and barbed wire during the war, known as Palace Internment Camp.
Copyright Lily Publishing, with permission.

Douglas: Sefton Camp

This camp, based on the Sefton Hotel on Harris Promenade and Church Road, is thought to have been used mainly for German and Austrian internees from November 1940 to March 1941. The hotel and other properties were returned to the owners on May 4th 1941. Dedicated camp paper money tokens appear to have been used and seven issues of a camp paper were produced called the "Sefton Review". Items from this camp are scarce.

275	1940	SEFTON INTERNMENT CAMP / No. / DOUGLAS, I.O.M. dated d/o	Violet	H
276	1940	INDEX OFFICE / SEFTON INTERNMENT CAMP / DOUGLAS I.O.M. box h/s	Black	I
277	1940	SEFTON INTERNMENT CAMP, / ACCOUNTS OFFICE. s/l h/s	Violet	H
278	1940	Internee drawn or duplicated postcard.	N/A	I

275

```
INDEX OFFICE
SEFTON INTERNMENT CAMP
DOUGLAS I.O.M.
```

276

SEFTON INTERNMENT CAMP,
ACCOUNTS OFFICE.

277

278

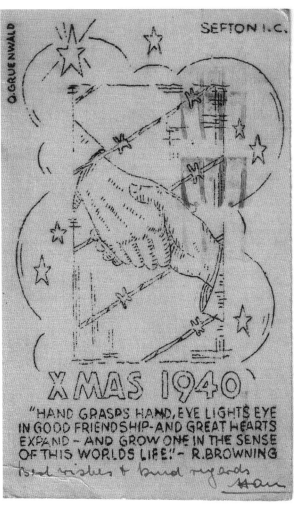

278

Plate 12: A coloured photographic postcard of Harris Promenade, Douglas showing the Sefton Hotel as it was just before WW II.

Plate 13: An enlargement of part of a photographic postcard of Ramsey showing the isolated nature of the group of buildings (centre) that formed the Mooragh Camp in WW II.

Ramsey: Mooragh (N, L or F Camp)

This camp was situated on the Promenade of North Ramsey near to the Mooragh Park in a group of thirty boarding houses, used both for accommodation and administration. It was the first internment camp to be opened on the Isle of Man. It came into use on 27th May 1940 and closed on 18th August 1945. At first the camp housed German internees, however, when camps in Douglas were closed, Italian and Finnish internees were sent to Mooragh Camp. It may also have housed Japanese internees. The camp codes given to the camp were; L for Germans, F for Finns and N for Italians, but to date items bearing the code L have not been seen. It may be that at a local level some mail received the code N whatever the nationality of the sender or recipient.

279	1940	MOORAGH CAMP Box h/s	Black	H
280	1940	MOORAGH INTERNMENT CAMP fat letters s/l h/s	Black	G
280a	1940	MOORAGH, INTERNMENT CAMP fat letters with comma s/l h/s	Red/black	G
281	1940	MOORAGH INTERNMENT CAMP thin, taller letters s/l h/s	Black/blue	G
282	1940	INTERNMENT CAMP "N" / REC'D small letters two line dated h/s	Red	I
282a	1941	CAMP N / ISLE OF MAN 2/l	Violet	I
283	1941	MOORAGH INTERNMENT CAMP/ No. / RAMSEY, I.O.M. dated d/o	Blue/violet	H
284	1942	R.F. CAMP / ISLE OF MAN Boxed cachet	Violet	I
285	1942	CAMP / I.O.M. dated double edge box h/s	Red/black?	I
286	1942	LETTER SENT WITH / SPECIAL PERMISSION / OF/ COMMANDER N INTERNMENT / CAMP box hex.	Red/violet	I
287	1942?	MOORAGH INTERNMENT CAMP / RAMSEY s/c	Red	H
288	1943	MOORAGH CAMP/ ISLE OF MAN / GUARD COY. ORDERLY ROOM d/o	Violet	I
289	1944	Postal stationery printed buff envelope On His Majesty's Service / Mooragh Internment Camp, / RAMSEY, I.o.M.	Black	G
290	1940	Internee drawn or duplicated postcard	N/A	I

MOORAGH INTERNMENT CAMP

279   280

MOORAGH,INTERNMENT CAMP   MOORAGH INTERNMENT CAMP

280a   281

CAMP N
ISLE OF MAN.

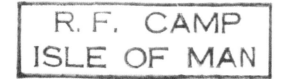

282   282a   283

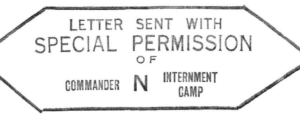

284   285

286

287   288

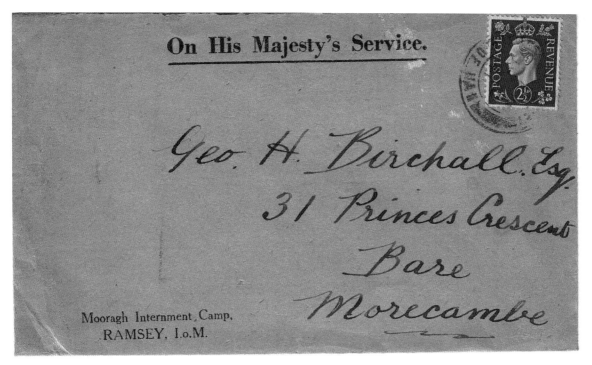

289

290

Peel: Peveril (M Camp British detainees, X Camp Alien detainees)

This camp was based on a group of boarding houses and others near Peel Promenade and overlooking the bay to the north end of the city. At first, from its opening during August 1940, it was used mainly for internees. During April 1941 these were sent to Mooragh Camp in Ramsey to be replaced by British and Alien Fascists on 12th May 1941. The Metropolitan Police took over guard duties from September 1941. By its closure in 1945 the Fascists had been joined by more internees, transferred from Douglas camps. Medical facilities were provided in Peel for internees at the facility called Ballaquane Internment Hospital, which was given the code ZR. Partly situated in a large building on the headland to the north of the city. Possibly a house or houses on Peveril Terrace may have been used for medical purposes.

291	1940	PEVERIL INT: CAMP/ PEEL 24mm s/c	Violet	G
292	1940	PEVERIL INT. CAMP / -PEEL- 28mm s/c	Violet	G
293	1940	PEVERIL INTERNMENT CAMP / No. / PEEL I.O.M. dated d/o	Violet/red	G
294	1943	METROPOLITAN POLICE / PEVERIL CAMP / x PEEL I.O.M. x dated d/o	Violet/red	G
295	1945	PEVERIL CAMP / x PEEL I.O.M. x dated d/o	Violet/black	G
296	1942	OPENED BY/ INTELLIGENCE OFFICER/ CAMP X box h/s	Black	H
297	1941	LETTER SENT WITH/ SPECIAL PERMISSION/ OF/ COMMANDER PEVERIL INT. CAMP box hex	Violet/red	I
297m	1941	LETTER SENT WITH/ SPECIAL PERMISSION/ OF/ COMMANDER "M" CAMP box hex	Violet/red	I
297x	1941	LETTER SENT WITH/ SPECIAL PERMISSION/ OF/ COMMANDER "X" CAMP box hex	Violet/red	I
298	1941	"M" CAMP 32mm s/c	Violet	I
299	1941	"X" CAMP 33mm s/c	Violet	I
300	1945	PEVERIL / CAMP dated d/c	Violet	H
301	1945	PEVERIL s/l h/s	Violet	H
302	1941	NOT / AT / PEVERIL / CAMP box hex	Violet	H
303	1940	NOT PEEL s/l h/s	Violet	H
304	1941	CHIEF POSTAL CENSOR s/l h/s (May not have been applied at Peveril)	Violet	G
305	1940	Internee drawn or duplicated postcard	N/A	I
305a	1940	Photograph of Peel internees / guards	N/A	I

291

292

293

294

295

OPENED BY
INTELLIGENCE OFFICER
CAMP X.

296

LETTER SENT WITH
SPECIAL PERMISSION
OF
COMMANDER PEVERIL INT. CAMP

297

LETTER SENT WITH
SPECIAL PERMISSION
OF
COMMANDER "M" CAMP

297m

LETTER SENT WITH
SPECIAL PERMISSION
OF
COMMANDER "X" CAMP

297x

298   299

300

PEVERIL

301

302

NOT PEEL   CHIEF POSTAL CENSOR

303   304

305

Peel: Ballaquane Internment Hospital (ZR Camp)

306　1943　BALLAQUANE INTERNMENT HOSPITAL / No/　　　Violet　　　H
　　　　　　ISLE OF MAN dated d/o

307　1943?　............../ Lieut-Colonel, / Officer Commanding Hospital　Violet　　　G
　　　　　　3/l h/s

　　　　　　　　　　　　　　· ·
　　　　　　　　　　　　　　Lieut-Colonel,
　　　　　　　　　　　　　　Officer Commanding Hospital.

306　　　　　　　　　　　　　307

Plate 14: Peveril Terrace, part of Peveril Camp during the war. It is thought that one of the houses was used as a medical centre, later to be transferred to a larger house on the cliff top north of Peel called Ballaquane Internment Hospital.

Plate 15: The Peveril Guard football team made up of Camp officers during the war, clearly proud to be Medal Winners.

Plate 16: A postcard of the Guest House taken in the 1930s which was to become
Ballaquane Internment Hospital, situated on the cliff top
at the north end of Peel overlooking the bay and Peel Castle.

Plate 17: Internees in the lounge of Ballaquane Internment Hospital together with the late Douglas Borough
Alderman, Ernest H. Ackery, then Medical Orderly Sergeant. "Courtesy of The Leece Museum".

Plate 18: A photographic postcard of Port Erin showing the cliff top hotels and guest houses that formed part of the Rushen Camp in WW II.

Plate 19: A photographic postcard of the promenade and bay at Port St Mary prior to WW II. The area formed part of the Rushen Camp.

Rushen: Port Erin & Port St Mary (Women W Camp, Married Couples Y Camp)

This camp, which came into use on 30th May 1940 and closed on 5th September 1945 was under the authority of the Home Office rather than the military. It was situated in a large area in the south of the Island in and around Port Erin and Port St Mary. Women, children, married couples and some "special" Germans, thought to have been consular officials unable to return to Germany at the commencement of hostilities, were interned in boarding houses and other properties used both for accommodation and administration. Port St Mary was used for married couples until August 1942 when on the 19th they were transferred to Port Erin where they remained until October 1944. Manx civilians living in the area continued to live and work as normal and some families took in internees. Passes for movement of both residents and internees in and around the area were provided by the Manx Police. Near Cregneash the R.A.F. manned a radar installation related to the protection of the "Western Approaches".

310	1940	WOMEN'S INTERNMENT CAMP,/ ISLE-OF-MAN Dated Bx h/s	Black	F
311	1941	WOMEN'S INTERNMENT CAMP/ ISLE-OF-MAN Dated Bx h/s serif lower letters	Black	F
312	1940	RUSHEN/ INTERNMENT CAMP/ WOMEN/ ISLE-OF-MAN Dated Bx h/s	Black	F
313	1941	WOMEN'S INTERNMENT CAMP/ SECTION/ A/ *PORT ERIN* t/o	Black	H
314	1941	RUSHEN INTERNMENT CAMP/ SECTION/ B/ *PORT ERIN* t/o	Black	H
314a	1941	WOMEN'S INTERNMENT CAMP/ SECTION/ B/ *PORT ERIN* t/o	Black	H
315	1941	RUSHEN INTERNMENT CAMP/ SECTION/ C/ *PORT ERIN* t/o	Black	H
316	1941	MARRIED ALIENS INTERNMENT / HEADQUARTERS/ *CAMP, PORT ST. MARY* t/o	Blue	H
317	1943	MARRIED ALIENS' INTERNMENT / HEADQUARTERS/ *CAMP, PORT ERIN* t/o	Blue-green	H
318	1941	HEADQUARTERS/ PORT ERIN/ ISLE OF MAN/ WOMEN'S INTERNMENT CAMP dated t/o	Red	H
319	1940	WOMEN'S INTERNMENT CAMP/ ACCOUNTS DEPT./ *PORT ERIN* t/o	Black/ blue	H
320	1941	PERMISSION TO SEND AIR MAIL / FOR COMMANDANT bx h/s	Black	H

321	1941	LETTER SENT WITH / SPECIAL PERMISSION / OF/ COMMANDER Y INTERNMENT / CAMP bx hex	Blue-green	I
322	1942	LETTER SENT WITH / SPECIAL PERMISSION / OF/ COMMANDER W INTERNMENT / CAMP bx hex	Red	I
323	1940	RELEASED BY / CENSOR bx h/s	Blue-black /violet	G
324	1941	Postal stationery envelope printed with <u>RUSHEN INTERNMENT CAMP</u> / POSTAGE / FREE	Blue/ black	G
325	1941	Postal stationery card printed RUSHEN INTERNMENT CAMP / Postage / Free	Black	G
326	1940	<u>ON HIS MAJESTY'S SERVICE</u> Postal stationery printed buff envelope with camp address	Black	G
326a	1941	<u>On His Majesty's Service</u> Postal stationery printed buff envelope with camp address	Black	G

<table>
<tr><td>310</td><td>311</td><td>312</td></tr>
</table>

<table>
<tr><td>313</td><td>314</td><td>314a</td></tr>
</table>

<table>
<tr><td>315</td><td>316</td><td>317</td></tr>
</table>

PERMISSION TO SEND AIR MAIL

FOR COMMANDANT

318   319   320

321

322   323

324

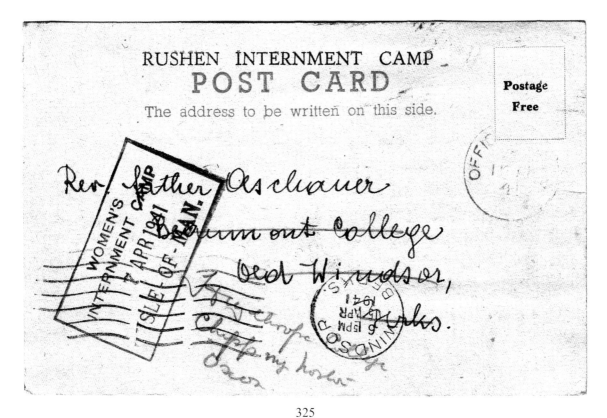

325

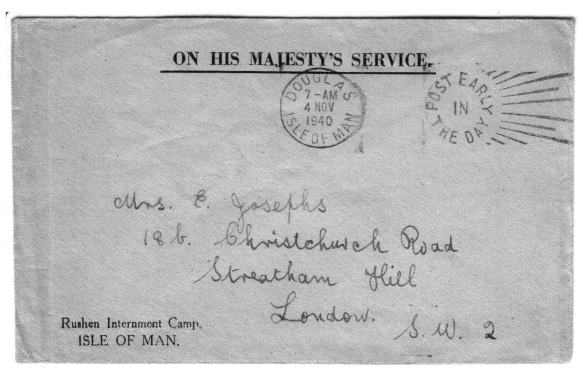

326

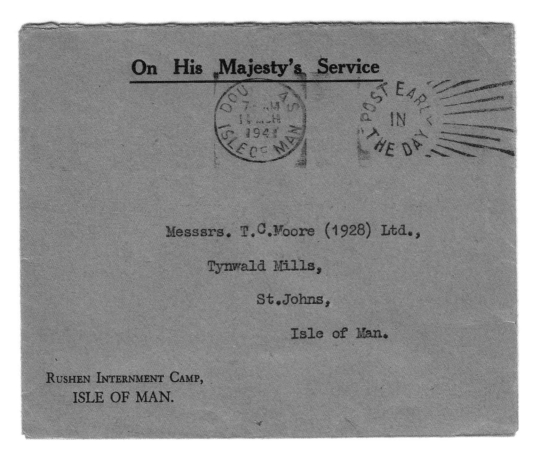

326a

Children from the camp school exercising on Port Erin Beach.

Police and Criminal Investigation Branch (CID)

The Police were responsible for the issue of various types of passes and other documents both to civilians, military personnel and internees. Such items often included a photograph of the person concerned as well as a Police cachet. Passes were required to enter and leave Rushen Camp and for military personnel stationed at Cregneash.

350	1942	C.I.D., ALIENS BRANCH / I.O.M. CONSTABULARY, DOUGLAS dated d/o	Violet	G
351	1941	CHIEF CONSTABLE'S OFFICE/ ISLE OF MAN dated s/o	Violet	F
352	1941	POLICE OFFICE/ CASTLETOWN ISLE OF MAN dated t/o	Violet	F
354	1941	POLICE OFFICE/ PORT ERIN dated t/o	Violet	F
355	1941	POLICE OFFICE/ PORT ST MARY dated t/o	Violet	F

350	351	352
353		354

Private mail without camp marks

Incoming mail to internees or outgoing mail without camp markings or examiner label	N/A	B

Transit Marks

These values are for marks without other camp cachets on plain covers or tuck-ins. If found with other marks of higher value, the higher value or values take precedence. As with correspondence in earlier conflicts it was possible to send mail between warring countries by way of a neutral country such as, during the Second World War, Spain, Portugal or Switzerland. Mail from allied countries then travelled through occupied regions to Germany and then was forwarded to its destination. At various stages the mail was subject to censorship and the authority handling it applied marks. In addition various postal jurisdictions might also apply hand stamps. The following list is by no means definitive but shows a range of marks most commonly found on mail travelling both to and from allied jurisdictions. As the war progressed mail routes changed to take account of prevailing circumstances and make a fascinating study.

360	1942	German Ab 20mm s/c Abwer h/s Also included in black machine mark with 7 lines	Violet/ red	F
361	1941	Ober Commando der Wehrmacht b 28mm s/c On cvr Camp Y to Guernsey	Red	E
362	1940	PASSED with crown coded bx oct	Red/ blue	C
363	1941	Nicht zu ermitteln./ Panzer Ubw. Erf.Abt.3 3 line cachet on cvr Peveril to Potsdam	Violet	F
364	1941	Geoffnet Ober Commando Wehrmacht / e s/l + 26mm s/c on adhesive lbl	Violet	D
365	1941	Geoffnet Ober Commando Wehrmacht / -b- s/l + 35mm s/c on adhesive lbl on cvr Camp Y - Lubeck Germany	Black	D
366	1943	CORREO AEREO / MADRID dated bx hex on cvr Camp Y to Guernsey 30mm	Black	D
367	1943	A.x. 20mm s/c on cvr Camp Y to Guernsey	Red	D
368	1942	UNABLE TO IDENTIFY. underlined s/l	Purple	G
369	1941	H.O. (B3.) INFORMATION BUREAU dated t/o	Purple	G
370	1940	3 – POSTAGE DUE 5 CENTS / Los Angeles, Calif.	Red	F/G

360   361   362

363   364

365   366   367

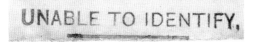

368   369

POSTAGE DUE 5 CENTS
Los Angeles, Calif.

370

First World War Postcards

During the First World War many printed and photographic postcards were produced both by internees and by local photographers. Some were clearly produced within the compound there being evidence that Knockaloe in particular had a printing shop. Many of the postcards are quite common, others less so. However because of their popularity amongst collectors they still command good prices at auction. Photographic images are often less common, indeed many are unique particularly if of individuals or small groups. Large group photographs, whilst very collectable, are more common. In this publication a selection of the main types to be found are represented though should not be seen as complete. Valuations usually range between F & H though condition and rarity together with postal markings, as always, will come into play.

Douglas Camp

Postcards from the camp in Douglas tend to be less common than those from Knockaloe probably due to the lower numbers of internees. As a result items from this camp have a premium, in particular those of individuals with special interest such as the one shown here of an internee who was a watch maker.

The Douglas Camp watchmaker.

During this period local photographers were permitted by the authorities to take photographs of individuals or groups and some either impressed their name and address in the corner of the photograph such as W. H. Warburton, Douglas or printed it on the reverse. Examples of the latter exist by D. Collister & Son, 29, Palatine Rd, Douglas. Internees with artistic skills designed postcards and often included their name in the design such as A. Rieger and G. A. Bredow. Another was G. C. Stoltz whose work may also be found on postcards from Knockaloe. In addition internees produced their own postcards, either painted or hand drawn, which are, as a result, particularly desirable and of course each one is unique. All postcards shown are from private collections unless otherwise stated.

1914

A printed Christmas postcard by G. Stoltz, date uncertain but probably 1914.

A printed Christmas postcard by G. Stoltz dated 1914. In 1994 the Castletown Philatelic Society reproduced this card as a dinner souvenir.

Internees Friedrich Schack No. 889, August Schonborn No. 929,
Reinhold Weiss No.927 & Willy Gille No.926, these names shown on the reverse
photographed by W. Warburton of Douglas.

A Christmas card, hand drawn and coloured by water colour.
Courtesy of Mannin Collections Archive.

A Christmas postcard in pale olive green on very pale green card dated 1914 Douglas
designed by G.C. Stolz.

A sepia postcard entitled "Erinnerung" or "Memories" dated 1914 - 19..?
showing a group of Internees in casual outfits.

A D. Collister & Son photographic postcard of the internee swimming group from Douglas Camp.

1915

The Catholic Chapel at Douglas Camp in 1915 postcard with Dean Crookall.

An Easter postcard of G. Stolz design.

A Whitsun postcard designed by A. Ellner.
Courtesy of Mannin Collections Archive.

A Christmas postcard by A. Rieger from Douglas Camp the printing in brown.

A Christmas postcard by A. Rieger from Douglas Camp the printing in brown.
Courtesy of Mannin Collections Archive.

A W. Warburton postcard of internees "Schitzschule" in front of the main building, Douglas Camp.

A Whitsun postcard from Douglas Camp, the printing in brown, by A. Ellner.

1916

A Christmas / New Year postcard by A. Rieger from Douglas Camp printing in black.
Also found printed in brown.

A Douglas 1916 Christmas postcard designed by G.A. Bredow (also seen in green).
Courtesy of Mannin Collections Archive.

A photographic postcard by W. Warburton of a group of internees from Douglas Camp entitled "Deutscher Turn-Verein Douglas Juli 1916".

1917

A Christmas postcard designed by G. A. Bredow dated 1917.
Courtesy of Mannin Collections Archive.

WW1 Postcards from Douglas Camp of uncertain date

A Christmas and New Year postcard hand drawn in black by pen.

A W. Warburton of Douglas photographic postcard of a theatrical group of internees at Douglas Camp.

W. Warburton of Douglas photographic postcard of an athletic group of internees at Douglas Camp.

Internees in the Douglas Camp Dining Hall photographed by W. Warburton of Douglas.

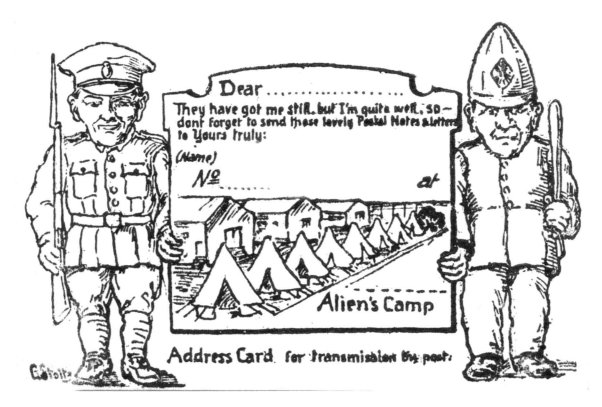

A line drawn postcard designed by G. Stoltz. Courtesy of Mannin Collections Archive.

A group of internees in front of the canvas tents photographed by W. Warburton of Douglas.

A postcard, numbered England 36, of the Boot Factory in which internees at the Douglas Camp worked. It was published by the Red Cross as one of a series showing the various activities undertaken in the Prisoner of War camps both work based and recreational.

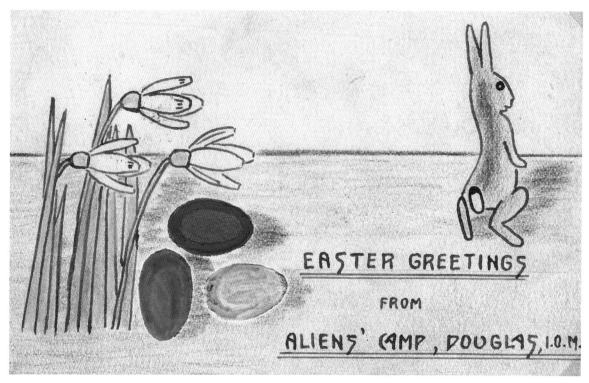

WW1 Internee hand drawn Easter Greetings postcard.

Knockaloe

1915

This postcard in blue showing a winter landscape was designed by A. Gensel, an internee in Knockaloe, one of a group of highly talented artists who between them produced a wide range of greeting cards. The printers are identified as S.K. Broadbent & Co. The text in German roughly translates as "Honour to God in the Heights and Peace on Earth, Cordial Christmas Wishes, the Camp Community, R. Hartmann, Pastor Knockaloe 1915" Pastor Hartmann was a priest who ministered to the internees and who seems to have been greatly respected. He managed to create a dedicated venue for his services.

This postcard, designed by A. Gensel and printed by S.K. Broadbent & Co. in blue, has been hand coloured in water colour by an internee. Some collectors prefer an item which has not been so treated and this can be reflected in the value, others enjoy the individual character produced.

An original drawing of Knockaloe Alien's Camp by prisoner B. Heinecke, dated 1915, on a postcard in sepia, produced by the Red Cross, headed England No.3.

These two postcards are both designed by G. Stoltz an internee artist whose works are frequently found, however the one on the left is more common than the one in blue on the right.

A local photographer D.W. Kees, working on Shore Rd, Peel, produced many photographs of individuals and groups of internees, his details are usually found impressed on the right side of the postcard, this one, in sepia, is dated 1915 with a code number 11478.

Photographic postcard by D.W. Kees, Shore Rd, Peel showing a group of Internees with arm bands with a code number 12006 with a card reading "Kriegsgefangene (Prisoners of War), 1915, Isle of Man".

Gymnastic display by internees.

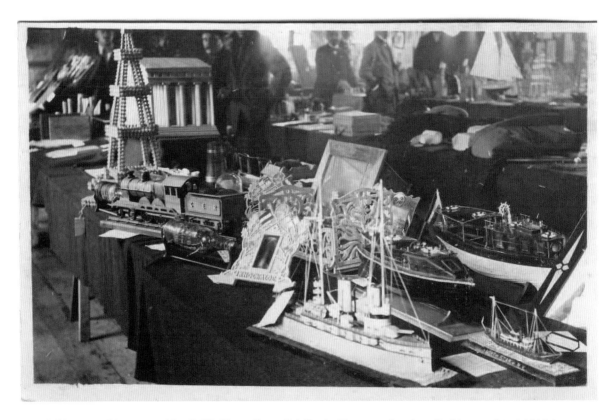

A Photographic postcard by D.W. Kees, Shore Rd, Peel of internee hand crafted items, dated 1915 in manuscript on the reverse. The internees had much time on their hands and making models, furniture and sculptures were popular ways of usefully occupying themselves.

A photographic postcard of a small orchestra of internees. Rehearsals for members of the group and arranging music by the musical director provided much to divert the players, also concerts given by such groups were a frequent feature of camp life raising funds by making a small charge to the audience. Programmes and tickets for such events are also collectable and give an interesting insight into life in the camp.

A hand coloured Christmas card dated 1915.

1916

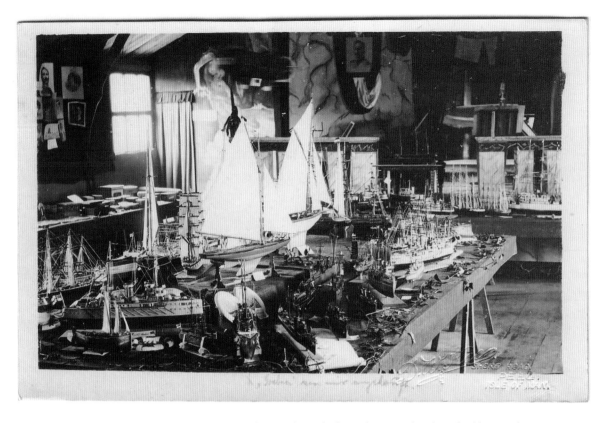

Two photographic postcards by D.W. Kees, Shore Rd, Peel, shows internee hand crafted items, the upper one dated 4-8/April/1916, Camp 3, comp'd 5 in manuscript on the reverse. The lower one showing the wide range of items made including a viola.

A Postcard of G. Stolz design "Easter 1916" and a photographic Easter Greetings postcard designed by A. Gensel published by D.W. Kees, Shore Rd, Peel.

Photo by D.W. Kees, Shore Rd, Peel. Male voice choir of Internees from Camp 1, dated 12/7/1916 shown in manuscript on the reverse.

Photographic postcard by D.W. Kees, Shore Rd, Peel showing internees with a dog.

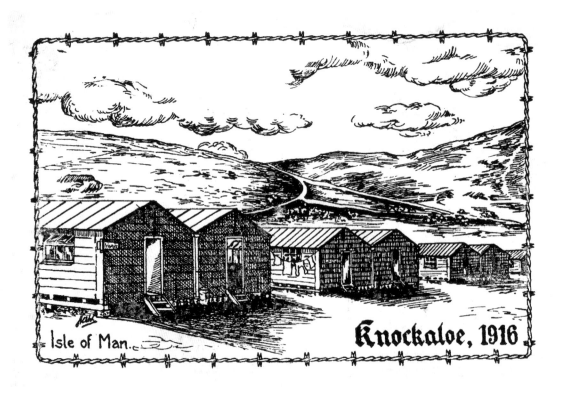

A line drawn or possibly etched postcard in black on white card dated 1916 showing camp huts.

Knockaloe - Camp 1 Post Office photographed during 1916. As well as dealing with mail from Camp 1 it clearly sold postcards and other artistic items to the internees. It is thought that each of the five Camps within Knockaloe had a small office dealing with post similar to this. The Camp also had a main central Post Office situated close to the railway line to and from which postal items were transferred between the smaller camp offices. By 1915 this central office had its own counter date stamp and dealt with a large quantity of letters and parcels.

A group of guards, who were stationed at Knockaloe Camp, all recruited from the Rushen area of the Isle of Man photographed in 1916. This photograph is published with the permission of Rosa Drown, the granddaughter of Harry Buckley Jones, who is seated last on the right in the second row, who was before and after the war postmaster at Port St Mary and who remained on the Island for the duration of the war.

A F. W. Kehrhahn designed Christmas postcard "Weihnachten Knockaloe I.O.M. 1916." showing internees
dreaming of their homes in rural Germany.

Weihnachten 1916.

Oh gold'ne Weihnachtszeit!
Mich zieht mein Sinn
Mit tausend Banden heut
Zur Heimat hin.

Mir strahlt im Lichterglanz
Ein Tannenbaum,
Der Mutter Weihnachtslied
Klingt mir im Traum.

Ich sinne träumend hin
In Sehnsuchtsqual - -
Von fern tönt Glockenklang
Es war einmal.

Max Horner.

A Max Horner poem included on a postcard designed by P. Czeczior for Christmas 1916
produced by the camp printing press Rotzler u Kirking,
showing a black figure or Christmas tree in the pale green vignettes.

Two postcards both designed by G. Stolz, black on white, the one on the left a Christmas postcard and on the right a New Year greetings postcard.

On the left an A. Gensel designed Christmas and New Year postcard in pale green dated 1916 and also a G. Stolz designed "Weihnacht 1916" and "Neujahr 1917" both with poetic inscriptions.

A photographic postcard of a hand drawn "Diplom" for singing by D.W. Kees, Shore Rd, and a postcard showing musicians at Christmas designed by H. Rottner, this example seen dated 1916.

A postcard black on white card designed by G. C. Stoltz for Christmas 1916 and New Year 1917.

1917

A postcard designed by G. C. Stoltz in black on a white card entitled "Heimat Fest" dated 1917. It highlights six activities undertaken by internees and illustrates each of them in appropriate costume. Sport, Theatre, Education, Art, Music and Handcrafts are illustrated together with a poem and a map showing Germany and its allies.

A postcard designed by A. Gensel with Easter Greetings from the Prisoner of War Camp, Knockaloe entitled "Ostern 1917".

On the left an Easter postcard designed by G. C. Stoltz in black on a white card and on the right a postcard dated August 1917 both with patriotic messages and wishes for freedom.

A photographic postcard of a small group of internees dressed for gymnastics by photographer D.W. Kees, Shore Rd, Peel.

A postcard, published by D.W. Kees of Peel, showing one of the championship football teams dated 26th May 1917. Clearly football was one of the popular sporting activities undertaken by the internees.

This Christmas postcard designed by W. M. Horner has been used by Isle of Man Post in the design of the Trench Art minisheet of 2014.

Postcards designed by E. Nettel such as the one shown here are less common than some, showing a group of internees gathered around a small Christmas tree entertained by a guitarist.

A Christmas postcard by an unknown designer in black and yellow dated 1917 and alongside, on the right, a postcard designed by G. C. Stoltz entitled "Pax 1917"
with good wishes for the New Year.

1918

Shown above are two postcards the one on the left welcoming in the New Year featuring the three legs of Man and a stylised view of the camp by the artist Emil Reichet, the other on the right with an inscription by G. V. Stoltz who has also created the one illustrated below entitled "Die Verwunsch'ne Insel" the text reflecting the artists longing to be gone from the Island.

This photographic postcard by Warburton of Douglas shows a small group of gymnasts outside one of the huts at Knockaloe. It is dated on the reverse September 1918.

A photographic postcard by D.W. Kees of Shore Road, Peel, showing the model village created by the internees which is similar in style to villages which would have been found at that time in Germany. The item is dated 14th May 1918 on the reverse.

WW1 Postcards from Knockaloe Camp of uncertain date

A Happy Easter postcard produced by the camp printing press Rotzler u Kirking camp 3 and G. C. Stoltz design black on white card Christmas postcard.

E. B. design cartoon type "Pech" and E. B. design cartoon type "Raucherei".

A C. H. designed cartoon type postcard "Pro Patria", a naive style item.

A Red Cross sepia postcard showing a small group of internees watching a chess match,
coded England No 28 – Knockaloe.

Katholischer Altar, Camp 4, Knockaloe, Isle of Man.

A photographic postcard by D. W. Kees, Shore Rd, Peel, showing the Catholic Altar in a dedicated venue for worship in Camp 4 with picture of Father Traynor who is thought to have visited the camp to take services.

A Douglas sepia postcard by W. Warburton showing a large group of internees watching a tennis match.

A photographic postcard by Warburton's of Douglas showing a group of three internees seated surrounded by items perhaps giving them some feeling of normality. Permission by Mannin Collections Archive.

A photograph of the entrance to Knockaloe Camp showing the railway line, a train, guards and the buildings along both sides of the entrance road (see map on page 10). Courtesy of Disused Stations website (http://www.disused-stations.org.uk/k/knockaloe/index.shtml).

An undated photographic postcard by D. W. Kees, Shore Rd, Peel showing internees with hand crafted items.

A photographic postcard by D. W. Kees, Shore Rd, Peel showing internees with cleaning equipment. In front of the table on the ground is a small label coded 1180-91.

A photographic postcard by D. W. Kees, Shore Rd, Peel showing a group of internee actors with a group on interested onlookers standing on the typical railway sleeper footpath.

This postcard entitled "Graves of the Aliens, Patrick I.O.M." shows the lines of internee graves. Sadly during the period from 1914 to 1919 several inmates from Knockaloe Camp were to die for various reasons. They were buried in Holy Trinity Church churchyard in Kirk Patrick village which is close to the Camp. In 1962 most were reburied at Cannock Chase, England, apart from some Jewish and Turkish internees who remain in their original resting place.

A photographic postcard by D. W. Kees Shore Rd, Peel showing the internee Catering Staff together with a Sergeant to the rear. Those working in the kitchens often brought with them the skills which they used in civilian life before the war. There is circumstantial evidence that some of those shown here worked in prestigious restaurants in England.

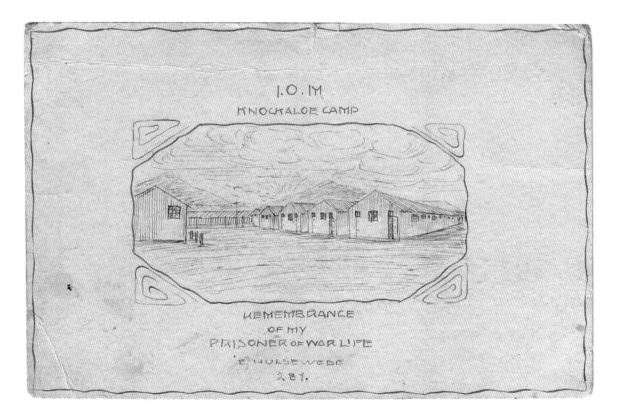

This line drawn postcard, by internee E. Hulsewede, has a picture which depicts some of the Knockaloe huts with hills and sun in the background entitled "Remembrance of my Prisoner of War Life".

WW1 Postcards from Knockaloe Camp of military interest

A photographic postcard by Stafford Johns, 2 Walpole Avenue and Little Switzerland, Douglas.
It shows a group of postal interpreters who worked at this camp.

A photographic postcard by D.W. Kees, Shore Rd, Peel showing a group of administrators, including
J. Madigan who was an Intelligence Officer at the camp, seated by the Knockaloe Interview Room.

Two photographic postcards by D. W. Kees, Shore Rd, Peel. The upper item shows medical orderlies, nurses and possibly Dr Stitt. The lower item shows Captain J. H. Cubbon, third from right, in the Quartermasters Office with his staff and internees and shows items manufactured by internees. The item is dated in manuscript on the reverse 1916.

Seen here two photographic postcards by D. W. Kees Shore Rd, Peel. The one above shows Lt. Colonel
Panzera, Commandant of Knockaloe and Quartermaster Captain Cubbon to the front at a Festive Day
(Col Panzera died on 4th June 1917). Below a postcard showing a Knockaloe Camp Inspection with
Commandant Lt. Col Panzera to the left of the group of officers.

Seen here are four photographic postcards by Warburton of Douglas. It is often the case that such portraits are difficult to ascribe, however these all bear the signature of the officer. Clockwise there is Lieutenant C. Radford who in 1915 was on duty at Knockaloe. By October 1916 he transferred to India near the Afghan border. Above right is Douglas Lieutenant A. M. Sykes also on duty at Knockaloe in 1915. By October 1916 he had transferred to India also near Afghan border. Below on the left is Lieutenant Claude Bibby. In July 1917 he became Captain and Assistant Sub-Commandant of No.2 Camp in Knockaloe. Finally on the bottom right is Dr George Keleman seen in 1915 who was in practice at Knockaloe. Unfortunately on 23rd September 1922 he died in a motorcycle accident.

Knockaloe Camp Guards Sports Day 1917 at the adjoining YMCA Field – Ref. 22.

Knockaloe Camp Guards Sports Day 1917 at the adjoining YMCA Field – Ref. 7.

Knockaloe Camp Guards Sports Day 1917 at the adjoining YMCA Field – Ref. 6.

Knockaloe Camp Guards Sports Day 1917 at the adjoining YMCA Field – Ref. 3.

Knockaloe Camp Guards Sports Day 1917? at the adjoining YMCA Field.
Courtesy of Knockaloe and Patrick Visitors Centre.

Lieutenants Freddy Evans, Brabant and Biggs

Major Lindsay, adjutant Knockaloe
(Earl of Crawford & Balcarres)
Courtesy of Knockaloe and Patrick Visitors Centre.

Two pipers at Knockaloe. Photo by Stafford Johns, Little Switzerland, Douglas.
Courtesy of Knockaloe and Patrick Visitors Centre.

Pictured in the centre of the postcard is Dr Robert Stitt of Fistard, Port St Mary who was in charge of the
troops guarding Knockaloe Internment Camp. Pictured with hospital orderlies and patients.

This rather distressed postcard of Internee Karl Topf with garden dated 1917 has a strange story to tell. British authorities made many copies of the original photographic postcard sent by the internee to his mother in Germany which were then dropped by air over the front trenches of the western front as propaganda. Several of them were in fact sent on to the original address much to the puzzlement of the recipient. Examples of this card are very scarce and usually bear traces of the muddy trenches they landed in. A copy of the reverse of the card is shown below.

This coloured postcard shows a portrait of Archibald Knox and a Knockaloe Camp scene which was recently produced by Manx National Heritage,
Courtesy of Manx National Heritage 2014.

This postcard was designed by the well know Manx artist Archibald Knox (1864-1933) and sent to Wilson James-Ashburner of Douglas, postmarked The Camp, Knockaloe, 22nd December 1916. It is known that Archibald Knox worked as a parcel censor at Knockaloe from November 1914 until October 1919. During that period his department handled 1,207,000 parcels. Courtesy of Mannin Collections Archive.

Second World War Postcards

During the Second World War the production of postcards by internees was of a different type to those produced in the First World War. More use was made of hand drawn and duplicated cards and the numbers produced appear to have been less than during the earlier conflict. As a result they are more difficult to access for postal historians. The reasons for this are open to speculation: postal censorship may have had a role as well as the convenience of new duplication methods. The outcome leads to increased scarcity and often higher values. As with items from the 1914-18 period values depend on rarity and condition and usually from the 1940-45 era start at G and may be higher if scarce or if a one-off hand drawn item. The following examples show a range of postcards and other items from this period.

Shown above are two postcards produced by internees, one entitled "PEEL 1940" designed by E. Fox - Kawe the other from Onchan Camp with the title "GREETINGS / Christmas 1940", for which the designer only leaves his initials K.F.M. Both the items are duplicated and then hand coloured on thin card.

Seen above are two postcards duplicated on thin card. On the left a Greetings card from Onchan Camp dated 1940 and designed by internee Kiewe, on the right a "XMAS 1940" postcard headed SEFTON I. C. designed by O. Gruenwald. A hand produced card dated 1944 from Hutchinson Camp is shown below together with an undated lino cut from Onchan Camp, both unsigned.

A Christmas card prepared in the Central Camp.

This duplicated and hand coloured Christmas card showing Onchan Camp and Santa with his sack of presents was produced by an internee who gives his initials F. Kl and is dated 1940.

WW2 Internment Camp Paper Money

During the Second World War the authoritics forbade the use of coin of the realm in internment camps. On the Isle of Man various methods were devised as a replacement. In the early days of the war camps used small ticket type vouchers or various coins which are outside the remit of this publication.   However there is evidence that various camp handstamps were used not only on mail but on other official items such as forms and paper money and for that reason are included here. The Home office issue of camp paper money came into use in 1941 but prior to this Onchan Camp issued its own notes of 2/6, 5/- and 10/-.

The notes which were produced for Onchan were thought to have been designed by the internee who became its bank manager until his release in 1941. The printer used for the issue was Phoenix Printing Co. Ltd., of Liverpool. They were printed on white Wiggins Teape paper with a watermark of a castle gateway, W T & Co, in script, EXTRA STRONG / 3009 in four lines. The notes are 120 mm by 170 mm in size and bear serial numbers from 0001 to 5000. Each of the three designs is shown below:

A mint copy of the 10/- Onchan Internment Camp note.

A mint copy of the 5/- Onchan Internment Camp note.

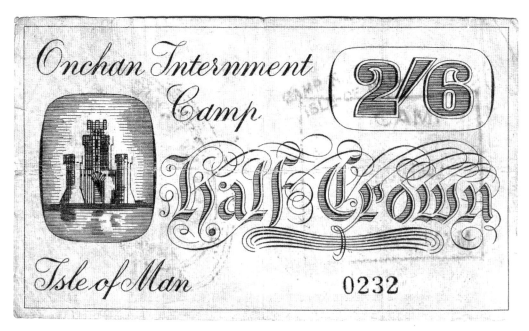

A well-used copy of the 2/6 Onchan Internment Camp note which received a dated double oval cachet of Granville Camp in red on the reverse. The mark, also used on mail, is numbered in this publication 231. On the front are two Mooragh Camp cachets 282a and 285, lightly struck in red.

Home Office Civilian Internment Camp Banknotes

During 1941 the Home Office made the decision to produce a banknote with one standard design to replace the unofficial camp currencies. Five denominations were printed:-

3d – Brown

6d – Red

1/- – Blue

2/6 – Green

5/- – Orange

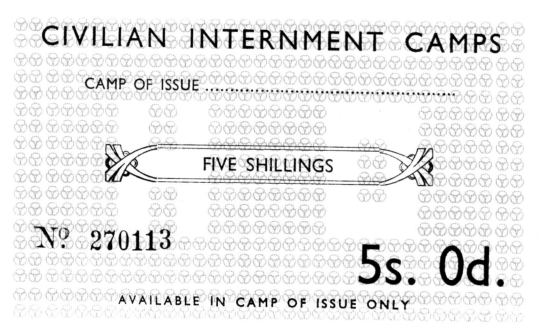

An un-issued 5/- banknote. Courtesy of Mannin Collections Archive.

In order to identify the issuing camp a hand-stamp was applied to the front of the note as shown in the examples below. As the notes were re-issued a dated hand-stamp was applied to the reverse or, as in some cases, to the front of the note. The notes were in use at all the internment camps in the Island, with the exception of Rushen Camp, until at least May 1945.

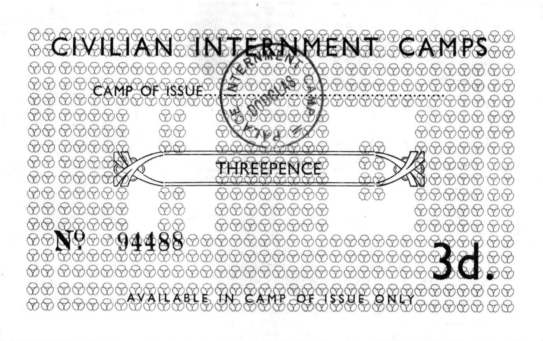

3d banknote issued at Palace Internment Camp, Douglas. Uses Palace cachet IOMPHS 265.
Courtesy of Mannin Collections Archive.

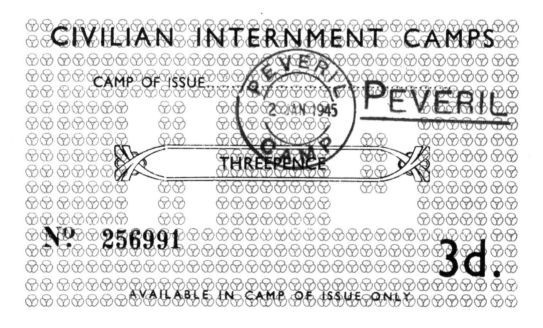

3d banknote issued at Peveril Internment Camp, Peel, dated 2nd January, 1945. Uses Peveril s/l cachet
IOMPHS 301 & d/c cachet IOMPHS 300.
Courtesy of Mannin Collections Archive.

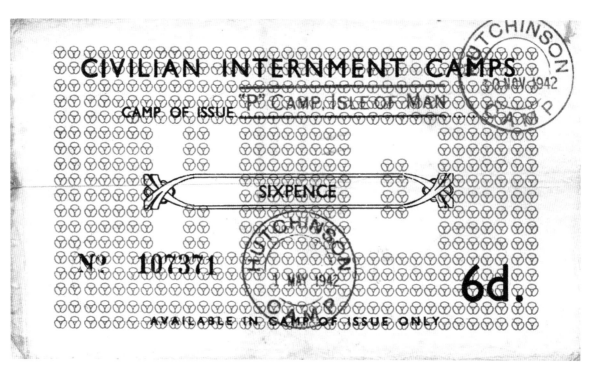

6d banknote issued at Hutchinson Internment Camp, Douglas, dated 1st May, 1942 and
then re-issued on 30th November, 1942. Uses new cachet IOMPHS 241.
Courtesy of Mannin Collections Archive.

1/- banknote issued at Mooragh Internment Camp, Ramsey. Uses Mooragh cachet IOMPHS 287.
Courtesy of Mannin Collections Archive.

2/6 banknote issued at Hutchinson Internment Camp showing dated hand-stamps for 1942 and 1943 as the note was re-issued. Uses new cachet IOMPHS 241. Courtesy of Mannin Collections Archive.

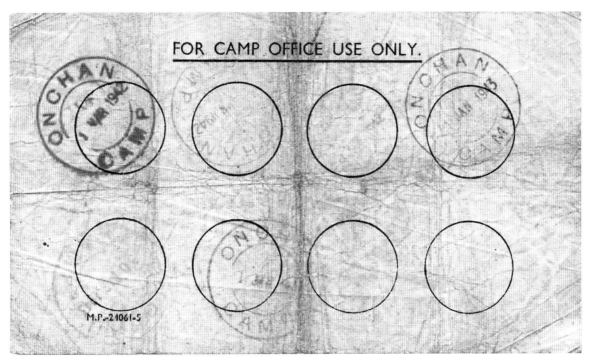

Reverse of 3d banknote issued at Onchan Internment Camp showing dated hand-stamps for 1942 and 1943 as the note was re-issued. Uses Onchan cachet IOMPHS 261. Courtesy of Mannin Collections Archive.

WW2 Location Maps and Road Closure Orders

The Isle of Man Government Public Records Office has an archive, accessible to the general public, of maps and documents which relate to the various Internee Camps on the Isle of Man. These documents show the location of the perimeter fences and access gates together with the properties which were to be used for the housing and administration of the internees. The maps are large in scale and for the most part line drawings showing the roads and houses affected. The camp areas are shown in various colours, the most common being pink. The maps are working drawings and the road closure orders are mostly typed and all are to some extent showing some signs of their age. However because they are of such interest and have never before been published they are included in the following pages.

The numbers shown in the text for the maps and documents relate to those given to them by the Public Records Office and apply to both the maps and the orders which in the archive are fixed together. All items in this chapter are published with the permission of Isle of Man Government Public Records Office for which the Isle of Man Postal History Society is most grateful.

Details of the Maps and Orders in this chapter:

Reference Number	Title
136-1940	Mooragh Camp, Ramsey
139-1940	Onchan Camp
142-1940	Central Camp, Douglas
239-1940	Palace Camp, Douglas
267-1940	Metropole Camp, Douglas
278-1940	Hutchinson Camp, Douglas
326-1940	Peveril Camp, Victoria Terrace, Peel
365-1940	Granville Camp, Douglas
366-1940	Sefton Camp, Douglas
372-1940	Peveril Camp, Peveril Terrace, Peel
377-1940	Rushen Internment Area
093-1941	Rushen Camp, Port St Mary
107-1941	Rushen Camp, Port Erin
030-1945	Peveril Camp, Peel
104-1945	Ballaquane Internment Hospital in Peel

ISLE OF MAN
TO WIT

By His Excellency Vice Admiral The Right Honourable
The Earl Granville, C.B., D.S.O., Lieutenant Governor of
the said Isle,   &c.,   &c.,   &c.

THE DEFENCE REGULATIONS (ISLE OF MAN) 1939.

CONTROL OF HIGHWAYS - MOORAGH, RAMSEY.

I, the said Lieutenant Governor, in exercise of
the powers in me vested under the Defence Regulations
(Isle of Man) 1939, hereby Direct that the highways or
rights of way coloured red on the plan hereto annexed,
passing through certain premises on the Mooragh in the
town of Ramsey and parish of Lezayre, appropriated for use
in His Majesty's service, or through land adjoining such
premises, shall be forthwith stopped up, and DO HEREBY
prohibit the exercise of any right of way, or the use of
any such highways

AND I DO HEREBY give authority to Bertram Edward
Sargeaunt, Government Secretary, to take all such steps
as appear to him to be necessary and expedient in
connection with the stopping up of such highways or
rights of way

GIVEN under my hand this 25th day of May, 1940.

Granville

Lieutenant Governor.

Mooragh Camp, Ramsey - Orders
PRO.136-1940.

Mooragh Camp, Ramsey – Map   PRO.136-1940.

ISLE OF MAN
TO WIT

By His Excellency Vice Admiral The Right Honourable
The Earl Granville, C.B., D.S.O., Lieutenant Governor of
the said Isle,   &c.,   &c.   &c.

THE DEFENCE REGULATIONS (ISLE OF MAN) 1939.

CONTROL OF HIGHWAYS - ONCHAN VILLAGE.

I, the said Lieutenant Governor, in exercise of
the powers in me vested under the Defence Regulations
(Isle of Man) 1939, hereby Direct that the highways or
rights of way coloured pink on the plan hereto annexed,
passing through certain premises in the village district
of Onchan, appropriated for use in His Majesty's service,
or through land adjoining such premises, shall be forthwith stopped up, and DO HEREBY prohibit the exercise of
any right of way, or the use of any such highways

AND I DO HEREBY give authority to Bertram
Edward Sargeaunt, Government Secretary, to take all such
steps as appear to him to be necessary and expedient in
connection with the stopping up of such highways or
rights of way

GIVEN under my hand this _14th_ day of _June_
1940.

Granville

Lieutenant Governor.

Onchan Camp - Orders
PRO.139-1940.

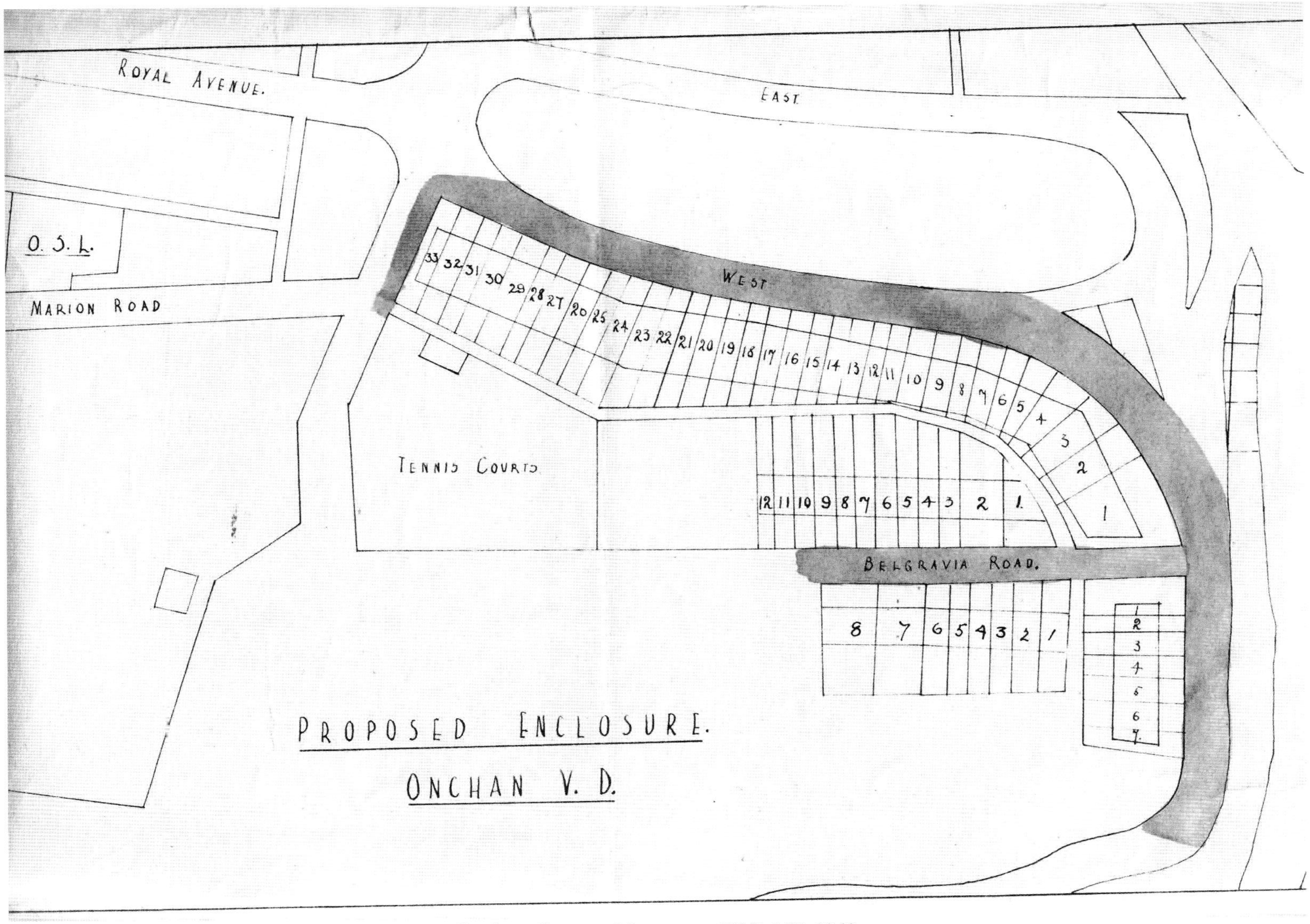

PROPOSED ENCLOSURE.

ONCHAN V. D.

ROYAL AVENUE.

EAST

WEST

TENNIS COURTS

BELGRAVIA ROAD.

MARION ROAD

O. S. L.

Onchan Camp – Map   PRO.139-1940.

ISLE OF MAN
TO WIT

By His Excellency Vice Admiral The Right Honourable The
Earl Granville, C.B., D.S.O., Lieutenant Governor of
the said Isle,   &c.,   &c.,   &c.

THE DEFENCE REGULATIONS (ISLE OF MAN) 1939.

CONTROL OF HIGHWAYS - CENTRAL PROMENADE DISTRICT, DOUGLAS.

I, the said Lieutenant Governor, in exercise of
the powers in me vested under the Defence Regulations
(Isle of Man) 1939, hereby Direct that the highways or
rights of way coloured pink on the plan hereto annexed,
passing through certain premises in the Borough of Douglas,
appropriated for use in His Majesty's service, or through
land adjoining such premises, shall be forthwith stopped
up, and DO HEREBY prohibit the exercise of any right of
way, or the use of any such highways

AND I DO HEREBY give authority to Bertram
Edward Sargeaunt, Government Secretary, to take all such
steps as appear to him to be necessary and expedient in
connection with the stopping up of such highways or
rights of way

GIVEN under my hand this *7"* day of *June*
1940.

Granville

Lieutenant Governor.

Central Camp, Douglas - Orders
PRO.142-1940.

Central Camp, Douglas – Map   PRO.142-1940.

ISLE OF MAN
TO WIT

By His Excellency Vice Admiral The Right Honourable
The Earl Granville, C.B., D.S.O., Lieutenant Governor
of the said Isle,   &c.,   &c.,   &c.

THE DEFENCE REGULATIONS (ISLE OF MAN) 1939.

CONTROL OF HIGHWAYS - PALACE TERRACE DISTRICT, DOUGLAS.

      I, the said Lieutenant Governor, in exercise of
the powers vested in me under the Defence Regulations
(Isle of Man) 1939, hereby Direct that the highways or
rights of way coloured pink on the plan hereto annexed,
passing through certain premises in the Borough of
Douglas, appropriated for use in His Majesty's service,
or through land adjoining such premises, shall be forthwith stopped up, and DO HEREBY Prohibit the exercise of
any right of way, or the use of any such highways

      AND I DO HEREBY give authority to Bertram
Edward Sargeaunt, Government Secretary, to take all such
steps as appear to him to be necessary and expedient in
connection with the stopping up of such highways or
rights of way

      GIVEN under my hand this 22nd day of June,
1940.

Granville

                    Lieutenant Governor.

**Palace Camp, Douglas - Orders
PRO.239-1940.**

Palace Camp, Douglas – Map   PRO.239-1940.

ISLE OF MAN
TO WIT

ROLLS OFFICE
- 9 JUL 1940
ISLE OF MAN

By His Excellency Vice Admiral The Right Honourable

The Earl Granville, C.B., D.S.O., Lieutenant Governor

of the said Isle,   &c.,   &c.,   &c.

THE DEFENCE (GENERAL) REGULATIONS (ISLE OF MAN) 1939.

CONTROL OF HIGHWAYS - CRESCENT, DOUGLAS.

I, the said Lieutenant Governor, in exercise of
(General)
the powers vested in me under the Defence Regulations

(Isle of Man) 1939, hereby Direct that the highway or

right of way coloured pink on the plan hereto annexed,

passing through certain premises in the Borough of

Douglas, appropriated for use in His Majesty's service,

or through land adjoining such premises, shall be forth-

with stopped up, and DO HEREBY prohibit the exercise of

any right of way, or the use of such highway.

AND I DO HEREBY give authority to Bertram Edward

Sargeaunt, Government Secretary, to take all such steps

as appear to him to be necessary and expedient in

connection with the stopping up of such highway or

right of way

GIVEN under my hand this 2nd day of July, 1940.

Granville

Lieutenant Governor.

#1.6

Metropole Camp, Douglas - Orders
PRO.267-1940.

Metropole Camp, Douglas – Map   **PRO.267-1940.**

ISLE OF MAN
. TO WIT

By His Excellency Vice Admiral The Right Honourable The
Earl Granville, C.B., D.S.O., Lieutenant Governor of the
said Isle, &c., &c., &c.

THE DEFENCE (GENERAL) REGULATIONS (ISLE OF MAN) 1939.

CONTROL OF HIGHWAYS - HUTCHINSON SQUARE DISTRICT, DOUGLAS.

   I, the said Lieutenant Governor, in exercise of
              (General)
the powers vested in me by the Defence (Regulations (Isle
of Man) 1939, hereby direct that the highways or rights of
way coloured pink on the plan hereto annexed, passing
through certain premises in the Borough of Douglas, appropriated for use in His Majesty's Service, or through land
adjoining such premises, shall be forthwith stopped up, and
DO HEREBY prohibit the exercise of any right of way, or
the use of any such highways.

   AND I DO HEREBY give authority to Bertram
Edward Sargeaunt, Government Secretary, to take all such
steps as appear to him to be necessary and expedient in
connection with the stopping up of such highways or rights
of way.

      GIVEN under my hand this 12th day of July 1940.

             Granville

        Lieutenant Governor.

**Hutchinson Camp, Douglas - Orders
PRO.278-1940.**

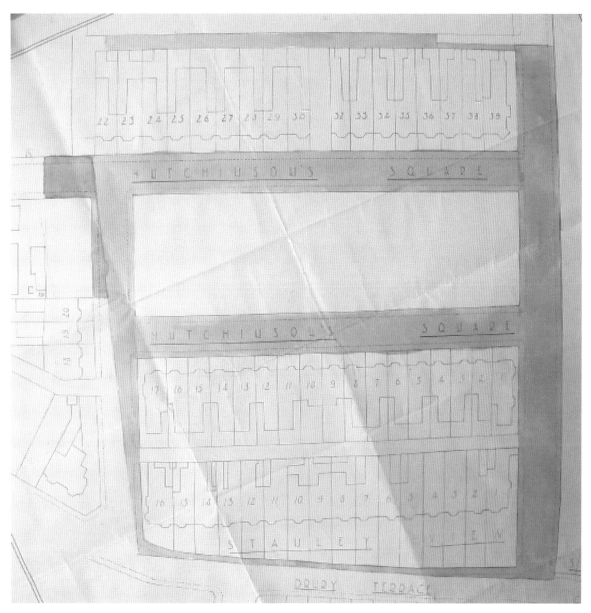

Hutchinson Camp, Douglas - Map
PRO.2/8-1940.

ISLE OF MAN
TO WIT

ROLLS OFFICE
30 JUL 1940
ISLE OF MAN

By His Excellency Vice Admiral The Right Honourable

The Earl Granville, C.B., D.S.O., Lieutenant Governor of

the said Isle,　　　　&c.,　　　　&c.,　　　　&c.

THE DEFENCE (GENERAL) REGULATIONS (ISLE OF MAN) 1939.

CONTROL OF HIGHWAYS IN THE TOWN OF PEEL.

I, the said Lieutenant Governor, in exercise of
(General)
the powers vested in me　by the Defence Regulations (Isle

of Man) 1939, hereby direct that the highways or rights

of way coloured pink on the plan hereto annexed, passing

through certain premises in the Town of Peel, appropriated

for use in His Majesty's service, or through land

adjoining such premises, shall be forthwith stopped up,

and DO HEREBY prohibit the exercise of any right of way,

or the use of any such highways.

AND I DO HEREBY give authority to Bertram Edward

Sargeaunt, Government Secretary, to take all such steps

as appear to him to be necessary and expedient in

connection with the stopping up of such highways or

rights of way.

GIVEN under my hand this *1st* day of *August,*1940.

Granville

Lieutenant Governor.

**Peveril Camp, Victoria Terrace, Peel - Orders
PRO.326-1940.**

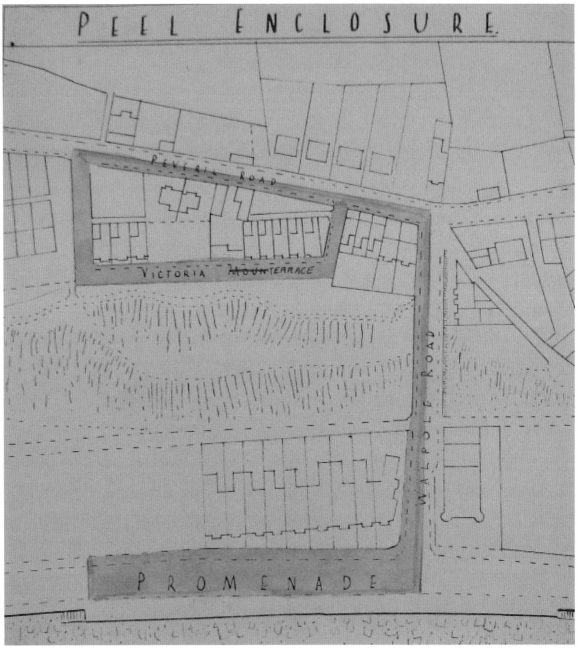

Peveril Camp, Victoria Terrace, Peel – Map
PRO.326-1940.

Government Circular No.
G.O.Reference No. 29749/83/2

ROLLS OFFICE
24 SEP 1940
ISLE OF MAN

Arms

THE DEFENCE (GENERAL) REGULATIONS (ISLE OF MAN) 1939.

CLOSING OF ROADS - LOCH PROMENADE, &c., DOUGLAS.

His Excellency the Lieutenant Governor has, under the
powers vested in him by the Defence (General) Regulations (Isle of
Man), 1939, made an Order, a copy of which is appended, stopping
up portions of certain highways and rights of way thereover in the
Borough of Douglas, being highways and rights of way through or
adjoining land appropriated for use in His Majesty's Service, such
highways and rights of way being coloured Brown on the plan annexed
to the Order, and including parts of the Loch Promenade, part of
Regent Street, part of Howard Street and part of Granville Street.

Failure to comply with the terms of the Order renders a
person liable to the penalties imposed by the Defence Regulations.
By Order.

Government Office,
          Isle of Man.   B.E.SARGEAUNT,
    21st September, 1940.   Government Secretary.

ISLE OF MAN
TO WIT

By His Excellency Vice Admiral The Right Honourable The Earl
Granville, C.B., D.S.O., Lieutenant Governor of the said Isle,
&c.,   &c.,   &c.

THE DEFENCE (GENERAL) REGULATIONS (ISLE OF MAN) 1939.

CONTROL OF HIGHWAYS - LOCH PROMENADE &c. DOUGLAS.

I, the said Lieutenant Governor, in exercise of the powers
vested in me under the Defence (General) Regulations (Isle of Man)
1939, hereby Direct that the highways or rights of way coloured
Brown on the plan hereto annexed, passing through certain premises
in the Borough of Douglas, appropriated for use in His Majesty's
service, or through land adjoining such premises, shall be forthwith stopped up, and DO hereby Prohibit the exercise of any right
of way, or the use of such highways.

And I Do Hereby give authority to Bertram Edward Sargeaunt,
Government Secretary, to take all such steps as appear to him to
be necessary and expedient in connection with the stopping up of
such highways or rights of way.

GIVEN under my hand this 21st   day of September 1940.

                         Granville

                    Lieutenant Governor.

**Granville Camp, Douglas - Orders
PRO.365-1940.**

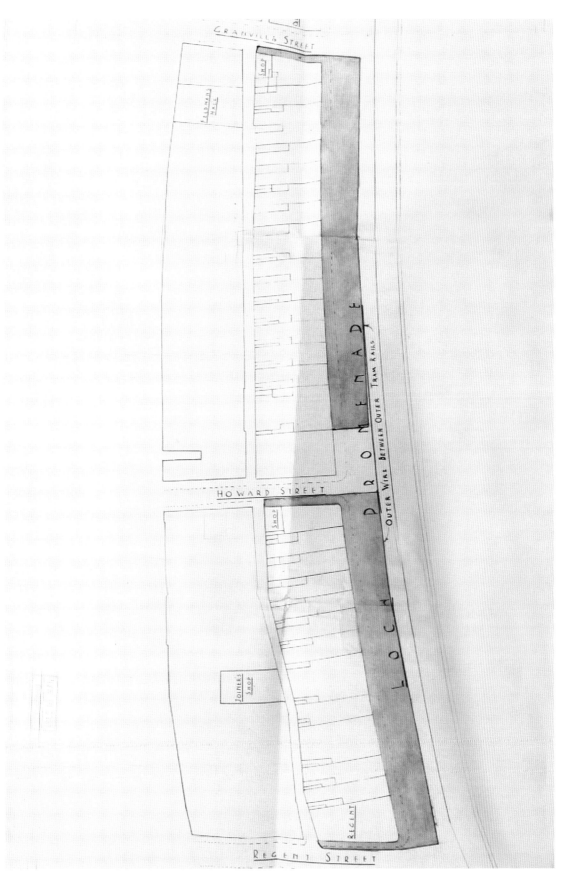

Granville Camp, Douglas – Map   **PRO.365-1940.**

Government Circular No.
G.O. Reference No. 29749/83/2

ROLLS OFFICE
2 4 SEP 1940
ISLE OF MAN

Arms

THE DEFENCE (GENERAL) REGULATIONS (ISLE OF MAN), 1939.

CLOSING OF ROADS - HARRIS PROMENADE &c, DOUGLAS.

His Excellency the Lieutenant Governor has, under the powers vested in him by the Defence (General) Regulations (Isle of Man) 1939, made an Order, a copy of which is appended, stopping up portions of certain highways and rights of way thereover in the Borough of Douglas, being highways and rights of way through or adjoining land appropriated for use in His Majesty's Service, such highways and rights of way being coloured Brown on the plan annexed to the Order, and including part of the Harris Promenade between Church Road and the point where the Sefton Hotel joins the Gaiety Theatre, part of Church Road and the roadway at the rear of the Sefton Hotel and the Gaiety Theatre running from Church Road up to the back door of Villa Marina.

Failure to comply with the terms of the Order renders a person liable to the penalties imposed by the Defence Regulations.

By Order.

Government Office,
    Isle of Man.
21st September, 1940.

B.E. SARGEAUNT,
    Government Secretary.

ISLE OF MAN
    TO WIT

By His Excellency Vice Admiral The Right Honourable The Earl Granville, C.B., D.S.O., Lieutenant Governor of the said Isle, &c.,   &c.,   &c.

THE DEFENCE (GENERAL) REGULATIONS (ISLE OF MAN) 1939.

CONTROL OF HIGHWAYS - HARRIS PROMENADE &c. DOUGLAS.

I, the said Lieutenant Governor, in exercise of the powers vested in me under the Defence (General) Regulations (Isle of Man) 1939, hereby Direct that the highways or rights of way coloured Brown on the plan hereto annexed, passing through certain premises in the Borough of Douglas, appropriated for use in His Majesty's service, or through land adjoining such premises, shall be forthwith stopped up, and DO HEREBY Prohibit the exercise of any right of way, or the use of such highways.

AND I DO HEREBY give authority to Bertram Edward Sargeaunt, Government Secretary, to take all such steps as appear to him to be necessary and expedient in connection with the stopping up of such highways or rights of way.

GIVEN under my hand this 21st   day of September
1940.

Granville

Sefton Camp, Douglas - Orders
PRO.366-1940.

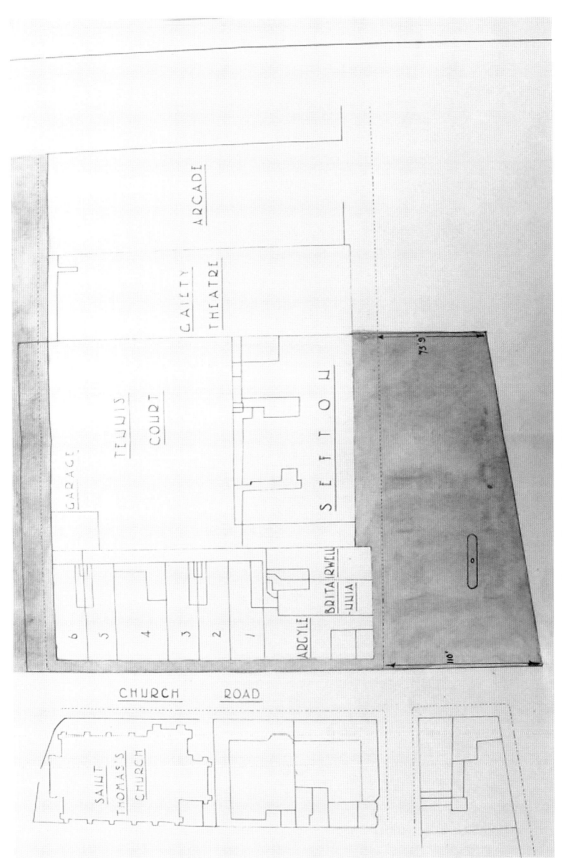

Sefton Camp, Douglas – Map   PRO.366-1940.

rnment Circular No.
Reference No. 29749/83/2

Arms

THE DEFENCE (GENERAL) REGULATIONS (ISLE OF MAN) 1939.

CLOSING OF ROADS

IN THE TOWN OF PEEL.

His Excellency the Lieutenant Governor has, under
the powers vested in him by the Defence (General) Regulations, (Isle of Man), 1939, made an Order, a copy of which is
appended, stopping up portions of certain highways and
rights of way thereover in the Town of Peel, being highways
and rights of way through or adjoining land appropriated
for use in His Majesty's Service, such highways and rights
of way being coloured brown on the plan annexed to the
Order and including Mount Morrison, Peveril Terrace, and
part of Peveril Road.

Failure to comply with the terms of the Order
renders a person liable to the penalties imposed by the
Defence Regulations.

BY ORDER.

Government Office,
Isle of Man.
2nd October, 1940.

B.E.SARGEAUNT,
Government Secretary.

ISLE OF MAN
TO WIT

By His Excellency Vice Admiral The Right Honourable The
Earl Granville, C.B., D.S.O., Lieutenant Governor of the
said Isle,   &c.,   &c.,   b&c.

THE DEFENCE (GENERAL) REGULATIONS (ISLE OF MAN) 1939.

CONTROL OF HIGHWAYS
IN THE TOWN OF PEEL.

I, the said Lieutenant Governor, in exercise of
the powers vested in me under the Defence (General)
Regulations (Isle of Man), 1939, hereby Direct that the
highways or rights of way coloured brown on the plan hereto
annexed, passing through certain premises in the Town of Peel
appropriated for use in His Majesty's Service, or through
land adjoining such premises, shall be forthwith stopped up,
and DO hereby Prohibit the exercise of any right of way,
or the use of such highways.
And I Do Hereby give authority to Bertram Edward
Sargeaunt, Government Secretary, to take all such steps as
appear to him to be necessary and expedient in connection
with the stopping up of such highways or rights of way.
GIVEN under my hand this 2nd day of October, 1940.

Peveril Camp, Peveril Terrace, Peel - Orders
PRO.372-1940.

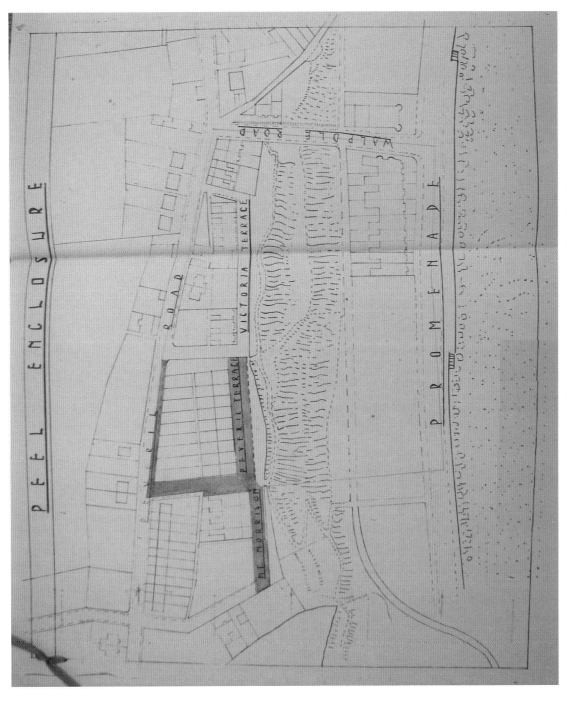

Peveril Camp, Peveril Terrace, Peel – Map   PRO.372-1940.

ISLE OF MAN
TO WIT

ROLLS OFFICE

11 OCT 1940

ISLE OF MAN

By His Excellency Vice Admiral The Right Honourable The
Earl Granville, C.B., D.S.O., Lieutenant Governor of the
said Isle,   &c.,   &c.,   &c.

THE DEFENCE (GENERAL) REGULATIONS (ISLE OF MAN) 1939.

CONTROL OF HIGHWAYS - PORT ERIN, PORT ST MARY AND PARISH
OF RUSHEN

     I, the said Lieutenant Governor, in exercise of the
powers vested in me by the Defence (General) Regulations
(Isle of Man) 1939, and all other powers me in that behalf
enabling, DO hereby make the following Order :

1.   All highways or rights of way leading to other parts of
the Island from an area comprising portions of the Village
districts of Port Erin and Port St Mary and Parish of
Rushen bordered pink on the plan attached hereto, shall be
forthwith stopped up and the exercise of any right of way
or the use of any such highways, is hereby prohibited
except that the following entrances may be used by authorised persons during the hours herein specified and where a
special purpose is specified for such purpose only, viz :

    The Four Roads (24 hours of the day).
    The Howe Road (24 hours of the day)
    Fistard Road (24 hours of the day).
    Spaldrick Hill (7 a.m. to 11 p.m. daily).
    Ballacreggan (7 a.m. to 11 p.m. daily).
    Darragh Road   ) (Open daily from 7 a.m. to 12
    Ballahane Farm Road) noon and from 3 p.m. to 6 p.m.
    Glendown Farm Road) if required in connection with
                         farming operations only).

2.   Authorised persons may only leave or enter the said area
by the said road entrances and then only between the times
and for the purposes set forth above opposite the same, or
by the Isle of Man Railway.

     AND I DO HEREBY give authority to Bertram Edward
Sargeaunt, Government Secretary, to take all such steps as
appear to him to be necessary and expedient in connection
with the stopping up of such highways or rights of way.

     This Order revokes the Order made by me on the 2nd
August, 1940, controlling highways and rights of way
leading from the area comprising the Village Districts of
Port Erin and Port St Mary and portions of the Parish of
Rushen to other parts of the Island, but without
prejudice to anything done or suffered thereunder.

     GIVEN under my hand this 11th day of October, 1940.

Granville

Lieutenant Governor.

**Rushen Internment Area - Orders
PRO.377-1940.**

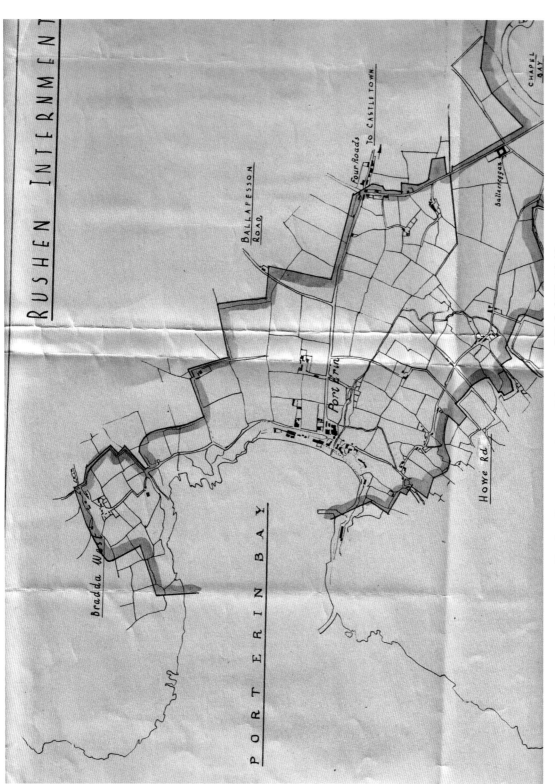

Rushen Internment Area – Map   **PRO.377-1940.**

ISLE OF MAN
TO WIT

ROLLS OFFICE

11 OCT 1940

ISLE OF MAN

By His Excellency Vice Admiral The Right Honourable The
Earl Granville, C.B., D.S.O., Lieutenant Governor of the
said Isle,   &c.,   &c.,   &c.

THE DEFENCE (GENERAL) REGULATIONS (ISLE OF MAN) 1939.

CONTROL OF HIGHWAYS - PORT ERIN, PORT ST MARY AND PARISH
OF RUSHEN

       I, the said Lieutenant Governor, in exercise of the
powers vested in me by the Defence (General) Regulations
(Isle of Man) 1939, and all other powers me in that behalf
enabling, DO hereby make the following Order :

1.   All highways or rights of way leading to other parts of
the Island from an area comprising portions of the Village
districts of Port Erin and Port St Mary and Parish of
Rushen bordered pink on the plan attached hereto, shall be
forthwith stopped up and the exercise of any right of way
or the use of any such highways, is hereby prohibited
except that the following entrances may be used by authorised persons during the hours herein specified and where a
special purpose is specified for such purpose only, viz :

    The Four Roads (24 hours of the day).
    The Howe Road (24 hours of the day)
    Fistard Road (24 hours of the day).
    Spaldrick Hill (7 a.m. to 11 p.m. daily).
    Ballacreggan (7 a.m. to 11 p.m. daily).
    Darragh Road   )   (Open daily from 7 a.m. to 12
    Ballahane Farm Road)   noon and from 3 p.m. to 6 p.m.
    Glendown Farm Road)   if required in connection with
                          farming operations only).

2.   Authorised persons may only leave or enter the said area
by the said road entrances and then only between the times
and for the purposes set forth above opposite the same, or
by the Isle of Man Railway.

       AND I DO HEREBY give authority to Bertram Edward
Sargeaunt, Government Secretary, to take all such steps as
appear to him to be necessary and expedient in connection
with the stopping up of such highways or rights of way.

       This Order revokes the Order made by me on the 2nd
August, 1940, controlling highways and rights of way
leading from the area comprising the Village Districts of
Port Erin and Port St Mary and portions of the Parish of
Rushen to other parts of the Island, but without
prejudice to anything done or suffered thereunder.

       GIVEN under my hand this 11th day of October, 1940.

                          Granville

                          Lieutenant Governor.

**Rushen Internment Area - Orders
PRO.377-1940.**

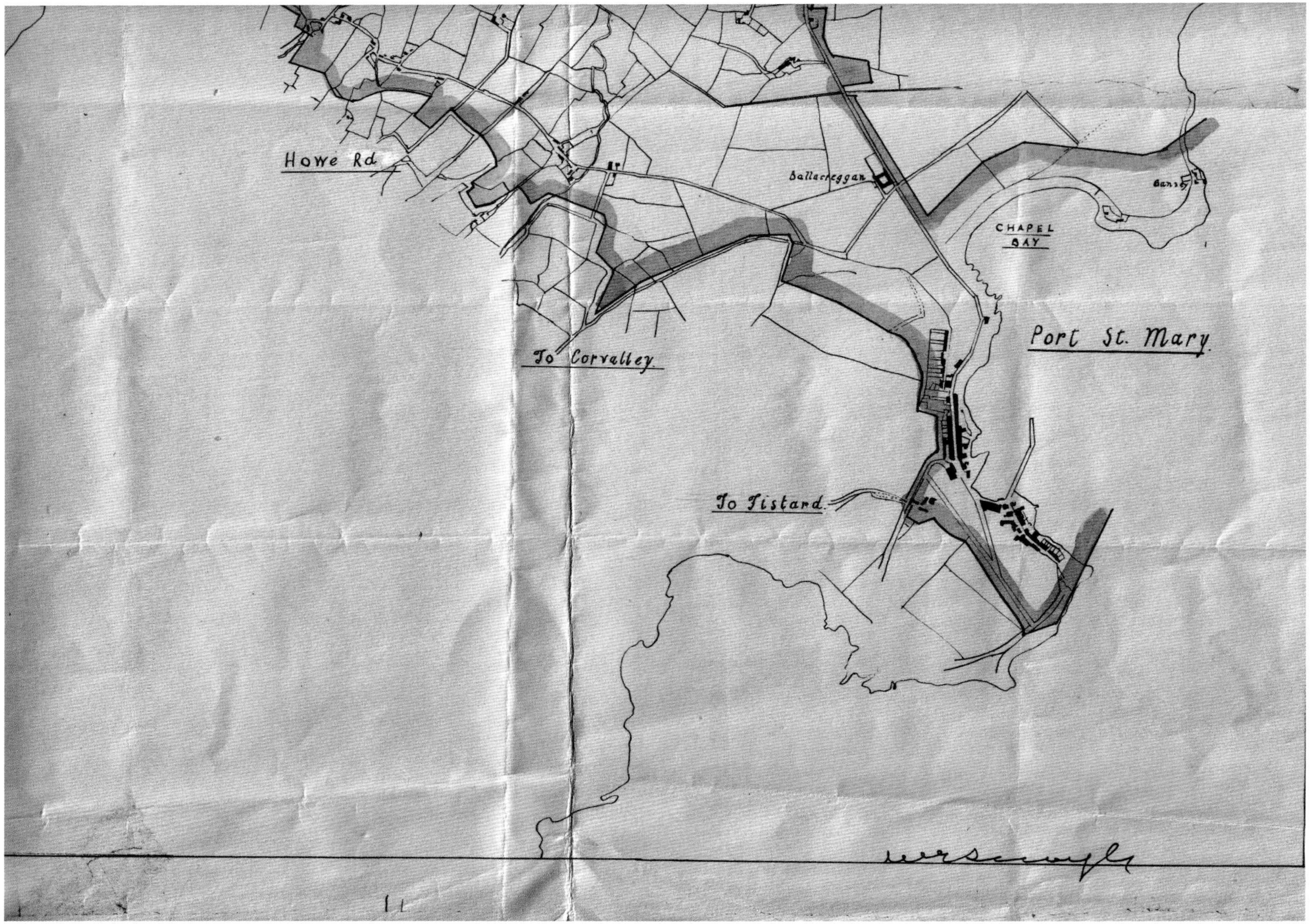

Port St. Mary.

CHAPEL BAY

Ballacleggan

To Fistard.

To Corvalley

Howe Rd.

Rushen Internment Area – Map   **PRO.377-1940.**

ISLE OF MAN
   TO WIT.

By His Excellency Vice-Admiral The Right Honourable The
Earl Granville, C.B., D.S.O., Lieutenant Governor of the
said Isle,   &c.,   &c.,   &c.

THE DEFENCE (GENERAL) REGULATIONS (ISLE OF MAN), 1939.

            CONTROL OF HIGHWAYS, PORT ST. MARY.

        I, the said Lieutenant Governor, in exercise of
the powers vested in me by the Defence (General) Regulations
(Isle of Man), 1939, and all other powers me in that behalf
enabling, DO hereby make the following Order :

1.   All highways or rights of way leading to other
parts of the Island from an area comprising portions of
the Village district of Port St. Mary coloured blue and
purple respectively on the plan attached hereto, shall be
forthwith stopped up and the exercise of any right of way
or the use of any such highways, is hereby prohibited except that the following entrances may be used by authorised
persons during the hours herein specified and where a
special purpose is specified for such purpose only, viz :

        Main Road (24 hours of the day).
        Promenade (24 hours of the day).
        Fistard Road (24 hours of the day).

2.   Authorised persons may only leave or enter the
said area by the said road entrances and then only between
the times and for the purposes set forth above opposite the
same.

        AND I DO HEREBY give authority to Bertram Edward
Sargeaunt, Government Secretary, to take all such steps
as appear to him to be necessary and expedient in connection
with the stopping up of such highways or rights of way.

        This Order shall come into force on the 7th day of
May, 1941.

        GIVEN under my hand this 5ᵗʰ day of May, 1941.

                              Granville

                    Lieutenant Governor.

Rushen Camp, Port St Mary - Orders
PRO.093-1941.

Rushen Camp, Port St Mary – Map   PRO.093-1941.

ISLE OF MAN
TO WIT

ROLLS OFFICE
2 0 MAY 1941
ISLE OF MAN

By His Excellency Vice Admiral The Right Honourable The

Earl Granville, C.B., D.S.O., Lieutenant Governor of the

said Isle, &c., &c., &c.

THE DEFENCE (GENERAL) REGULATIONS (ISLE OF MAN), 1939.

CONTROL OF HIGHWAYS, PORT ERIN.

I, the said Lieutenant Governor, in exercise of
the powers vested in me by the Defence (General) Regulations
(Isle of Man), 1939, and all other powers me in that
behalf enabling, DO hereby make the following Order :

1. All highways or rights of way leading to other parts of
the Island from an area comprising a portion of the Village
District of Port Erin bordered red on the plan attached
hereto, shall be forthwith stopped up and the exercise of
any right of way or the use of any such highways, is hereby
prohibited except that the following entrances may be used
by authorised persons during the hours herein specified,
and, where a special purpose is specified, for such
purpose only, viz :

Station Road (24 hours of the day).

Ballafurt Road (24 hours of the day).

Bradda Road (24 hours of the day).

2. Authorised persons may only leave or enter the said area
by the said road entrances

AND I DO HEREBY give authority to Bertram Edward
Sargeaunt, Government Secretary, to take all such steps
as appear to him to be necessary and expedient in
connection with the stopping up of such highways or rights
of way.

This Order revokes the Order made by me on the
11th October, 1940, controlling highways and rights of
way leading from the area comprising the Village Districts
of Port Erin and Port St Mary and portions of the Parish
of Rushen to other parts of the Island, but without
prejudice to anything done or suffered thereunder.
This Order shall come into force on the 7th day of
May, 1941

GIVEN under my hand this 5th day of May, 1941.

Granville

Lieutenant Governor.

**Rushen Camp, Port Erin - Orders
PRO.107-1941.**

Rushen Camp, Port Erin – Map   PRO.107-1941.

Government Circular No. 3807.
G.O. Reference No. 29749/83/5.

ROLLS OFF
28 FE
ISLE OF M

The Defence (General) Regulations (Isle of Man), 1939.

RE-OPENING OF PEVERIL ROAD, PEEL.

His Excellency the Lieutenant Governor has made an Order under the Defence Regulations repealing and re-enacting in a modified form the Order made by him on the 12th May, 1941, directing the closing of certain highways and rights of way in Peel.

The effect of the new Order is to re-open part of Peveril Road so that this thoroughfare will again be available for pedestrians and for vehicular traffic. By the terms of an Order contained in Government Circular No. 3806, however, vehicular traffic may not proceed along Peveril Road in an upwards direction from its junction with Walpole Road to its junction with Fenella Terrace.

The Order comes into force on 24th February, 1945.

Failure to comply with the terms of the Order renders a person liable to the penalties imposed by the Defence Regulations.

Government Office,

Isle of Man.

17th February, 1945,

By Order,

J. N. PANES,

Government Secretary.

ISLE OF MAN
To WIT.

BY HIS EXCELLENCY VICE-ADMIRAL THE RIGHT HONOURABLE THE EARL GRANVILLE, C.B., D.S.O., LIEUTENANT GOVERNOR OF THE SAID ISLE,   &c.,   &c.,   &c.

THE DEFENCE (GENERAL) REGULATIONS (ISLE OF MAN), 1939.

CONTROL OF HIGHWAYS IN THE TOWN OF PEEL.

I, the said Lieutenant Governor, in exercise of the powers vested in me by the Defence (General) Regulations (Isle of Man), 1939, hereby direct that the highways or rights of way coloured green on the plan hereto annexed, passing through certain premises in the Town of Peel, appropriated for use in His Majesty's Service, or through land adjoining such premises, shall be stopped up, and DO HEREBY Prohibit the exercise of any right of way, or the use of any such highways.

AND I DO HEREBY give authority to JOHN NELSON PANES, Government Secretary, to take all such steps as appear to him to be necessary and expedient in connection with the stopping up of such highways or rights of way.

AND FURTHER I DO HEREBY revoke the Order made by me on the 12th day of May, 1941, stopping up certain highways and rights of way in the Town of Peel.

This Order shall come into force on the 24th day of February, 1945.

GIVEN under my hand this 17th day of February, 1945.

Lieutenant Governor.

Wt. P. 1730.—50/2/45. Printed (by Authority) by Victoria Press. Ltd.

Peveril Camp, Peel - Orders
PRO.030-1945.

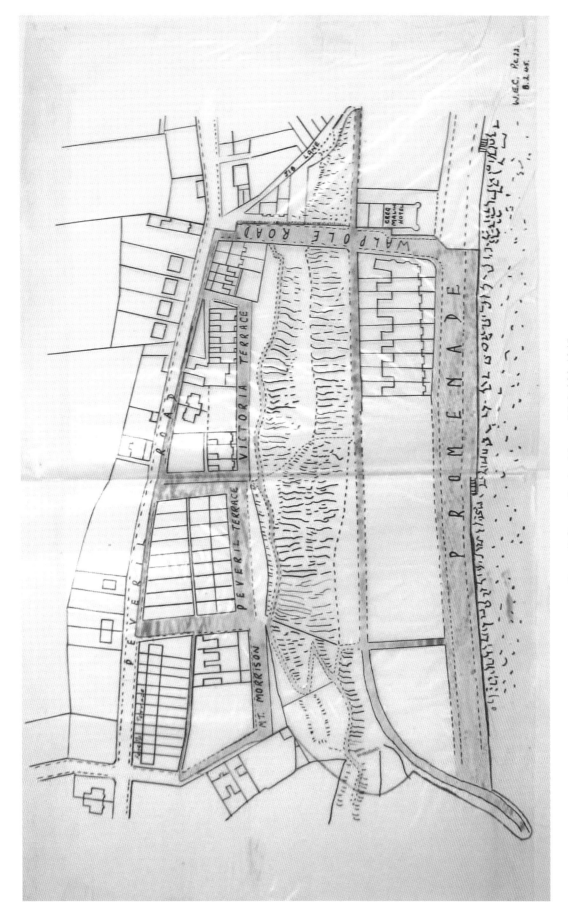

Peveril Camp, Peel – Map   PRO.030-1945.

OF MAN
TO WIT.

ROLLS OFFICE

23 JAN 1945

ISLE OF MAN

By His Excellency Vice Admiral The Right
Honourable The Earl Granville, C.B., D.S.O.,
Lieutenant Governor of the said Isle, &c.

THE DEFENCE (GENERAL) REGULATIONS (ISLE OF MAN), 1939.

      I, the said Lieutenant Governor, in exercise
of the powers vested in me by the Defence (General)
Regulations (Isle of Man), 1939, DO hereby direct
that the footpaths or rights of way coloured blue
on the plan hereto annexed, passing through
certain premises in the Parish of German appropriated for use in His Majesty's Service, or through
land adjoining such premises, shall be forthwith
stopped up and DO hereby prohibit the exercise of
any right of way or the **use** of such footpaths.

      GIVEN under my hand this 18th day of
January, 1945.

Granville

Lieutenant Governor.

**Ballaquane Internment Hospital in Peel - Orders
PRO.104-1945.**

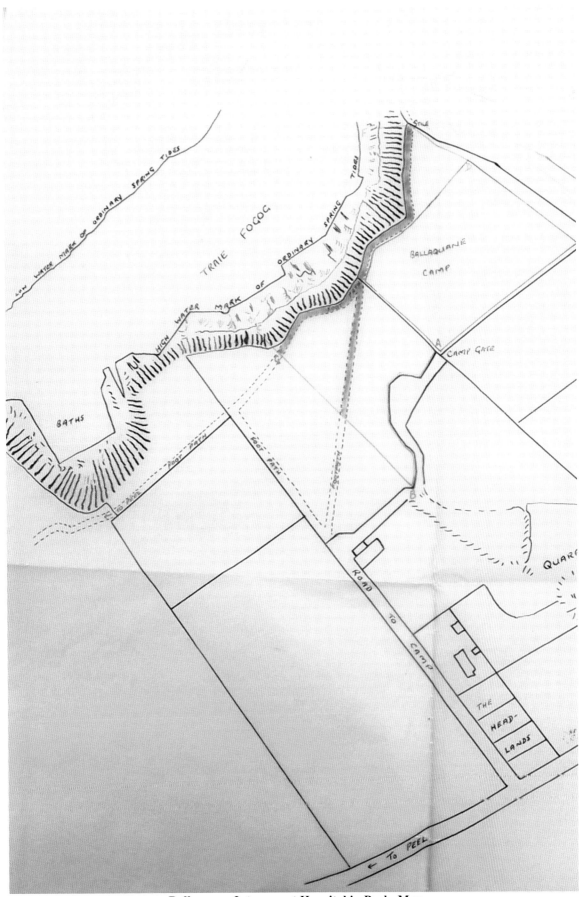

Ballaquane Internment Hospital in Peel - Map
PRO.104-1945.

Recent related Isle of Man Post issues

The Isle of Man Post Office has issued two commemorative issues in recent years which have an internment camp theme. These are the 2010 Internment Art issue and the 2011 Knockaloe Internment Postal History issue which are described below.

The 2010 Internment Art History issue

The Isle of Man Internment – Art History First Day Cover Cancelled Stamp Set was specially designed and released on 24th September 2010 to depict the wartime Internment Camps on the Isle of Man. These camps comprised of a series of guesthouses which held what is known as 'His Majesty's Most Loyal Enemy Aliens' who were foreign nationals that were separated from society instead of being imprisoned. The Isle of Man Internment – Art History First Day Cover Cancelled Stamp Set features six stamps representing 35p, 36p, 55p, 67p, £1.32 and £1.72 and features the full set of stamps cancelled with the first day of issue special postmark.

The issue 'Art History' concentrates on the fortuitous coming together of European artists who were interned on the Island during the Second World War. Known as 'His Majesty's Most Loyal Enemy Aliens,' these foreign nationals were separated from society, rather than imprisoned, and this unique concentration of talent in a handful of Manx guesthouses yielded a remarkable range of artwork that forms the basis of our stamp issue.

Under kindly captors a number of artists and musicians made the most of their time and some went on to become nationally and internationally famous in later life. Such artists as Kurt Schwitters, Martin Bloch, Ernst Eisenmayer and Hugo Dachinger developed their work to the sounds of the nascent Amadeus Quartet.

At the outbreak of the Second World War the Isle of Man was a major centre for civilian internment with the majority of those interned spending at least part of their internment on the Island. The decision was made to requisition rows of boarding houses and hotels along the promenades of several of the Island's resorts and their occupants were given one to two weeks to vacate their premises. The first camp opened on the 27th May 1940 at Mooragh Promenade, Ramsey. The internees came from a broad and diverse range of backgrounds and included many leading artists. The wide variety of artwork produced in the camps has provided an important visual legacy of what the camps looked like, together with an insight into the daily life of the internees and their concerns.

BERTRAM Three-Legged Postman 1940 - 35p stamp
Little is known of the artist, Betram, other than that he was a prolific artist who exhibited in the art exhibitions at the Onchan Camp, provided illustrations for the Onchan Pioneer camp newspaper and taught at the Onchan Camp School of Art. The postcard was sent as a Christmas card to Graham McKenzie, the local sub-postmaster, to thank him for the help and assistance he had given the internee camp postmaster.

HERBERT KADEN Peveril Camp, Peel 1940 - 36p stamp
Herbert Kaden (b.1921) was born in Dresden, Germany. His family were originally Jewish but had converted to Christianity. In 1938, Herbert and his mother came to Britain to escape growing Jewish persecution. He initially intended to be an architect but his studies were interrupted in 1940 when he was interned and sent to the Peveril Camp. He was released within a few weeks to work on a family friend's farm.

IMRE GOTH Life at Palace Camp, Douglas 1941 - 55p stamp
Imre Goth (1893- 1982), painter and inventor, was born in Hungary and studied in Budapest and Berlin. He became well-known as a portrait painter, particularly of members of the fashionable and glamorous Berlin nightclub scene. In 1935, Goth moved to Britain and through his friendship with the Hungarian film director, Alexander Korda, produced portraits of several leading British film stars. He was interned on the Isle of Man in the Palace Camp, Douglas from 1941 to 1942.

ERNST EISENMAYER Violinist at Onchan Camp 1941 - 132p stamp
Ernst Eisenmayer (b.1920), painter and sculptor, was born in Vienna, Austria. He was arrested and deported to Dachau in 1938 and following his release in 1939, he emigrated to Britain. Eisenmayer was interned in 1940 and held in various camps, including Onchan and Mooragh Camp (Ramsey) on the Isle of Man. He produced artwork for the Onchan Camp art exhibitions and the Onchan Pioneer camp newspaper. Following release, he became a toolmaker and then established himself as a sculptor, with work exploring issues of violence, oppression and abuse of power.

KURT SCHWITTERS Portrait of Klaus E Hinrichsen 1941 - 172p stamp
Kurt Schwitters (1887-1948) installation artist, painter and poet, was born in Hanover, Germany. Partly influenced by Dadaists, he created his own art movement in 1919 which he called Merz, which involved the creation of large scale art installations. His work was identified as 'degenerate art' and he fled to Norway in 1937 and then to Britain in 1940, where he was arrested and interned in Hutchinson Camp, Douglas. During internment, Schwitters produced several portraits of his fellow internees, together with collages and a Merz created out of porridge. The portrait of Dr Klaus E. Hinrichsen was painted gratis in acknowledgement of Hinrichsen's role as artistic impresario in Hutchinson Camp.

Acknowledgements
The Isle of Man Post Office would like to thank everyone who has provided assistance, guidance and permissions to reproduce artwork during the preparation of this stamp issue: The Ben Uri Gallery, Sarah MacDougall, Rachel Silman, Rosa-Maria Breinlich, Ernst Eisenmayer, Nic Hinrichsen and family, Manx National Heritage, Yvonne Cresswell, The Sayle Gallery, Dr. Isabel Schulz, Sprengel Museum Hannover, Kurt and Ernst Schwitters Stiftung, Jacquie Richardson and David Wertheim.

The 2011 Knockaloe Internment Postal History issue

The Isle of Man Post Office released a set of eight stamps and a minisheet on 8th August 2011 to document the postal history of the Knockaloe Internment Camp on the Isle of Man.

For the duration of the First World War there were two large camps on the Island: a requisitioned holiday camp in Douglas, holding some 3000 internees, and Knockaloe, a mile south of Peel, which was purpose-built using prefabricated huts and included its own railway link.

Almost 24,000 men classified as 'enemy aliens' were detained at Knockaloe with a military and civilian workforce of around 3,000 individuals looking after them. Many persons of note from the Manx community were employed, the most famous of whom was Archibald Knox, Manx-born artist and designer for Liberty & Co, London. From 1914 until 1918 he served at the camp as a mail censor. Another well-known figure was local politician Arthur Binns Crookall MHK & MLC, a caterer and philanthropist who was awarded the contract to feed some 28,000 people every day for the duration of the war, initially at the Douglas camp and later Knockaloe. The camps closed at the end of the War, the buildings were sold and Knockaloe returned to farmland.

Top Left Pair: Left Hand Stamp:
(Also, cover image of presentation pack)

The postcard issued by the YMCA is number 15 in their series and depicts the South Lancashire Brigade on Peel Harbour en route to the Army camp at Knockaloe Moar Farm in August 1908, the first year that mail was postmarked from Knockaloe. Other Regiments known to have attended this camp are the Royal Army Medical Corps and The King's Liverpool Regiment.

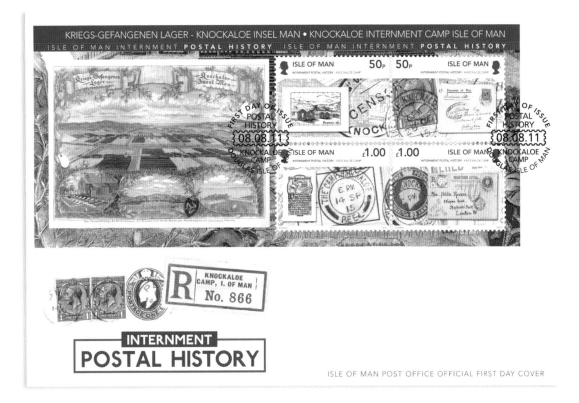

Right Hand Stamp:

The King Edward VII 1/2d first issued on the 1st January 1902 is cancelled by the 35mm Knockaloe Camp Peel Skeleton on the 3rd August 1908. The Skeleton was issued by the Post Office as a temporary mail canceller.

Top Right Pair: Left Hand Stamp:

The postcard printed by SKB & Co and designed by an internee depicts the general layout of Knockaloe Camp, together with a backdrop of Peel Castle and headland. Various trades carried out by the internees are illustrated on the card. It is dated 1915, thus issued within the first year of the Camp's operation and it sends "Greetings from the Prisoners at Knockaloe Camp, Isle of Man". This example has been hand coloured, as it was originally printed blue and white.

Right Hand Stamp:

The pair of George V Profile Head 1/2ds first issued in January 1913 are cancelled by the Code A Peel I.Of.Man Single Circle which looks to have been taken from the 1881 Peel D51 Duplex on the 23rd November 1914. The cover is an official Postal Stationery one titled "Aliens' Detention Camp, Knockaloe, Isle of Man" and, with agreement to open the Camp only being given on the 24th October 1914, this is one of the earliest surviving Internment Camp mail items known.

Bottom Left Pair: Left Hand Stamp:

The postcard was published by the Printers Workshop, Camp 3, Knockaloe Internment Camp to celebrate a Happy Easter during an unknown year between 1915 and 1919 when the Camp closed.

Right Hand Stamp:

The 3d King George V Registered Envelope first issued in 1912 is cancelled with two strikes of The Camp Knockaloe Peel Double Circle, datestamp 25th November 1915 and first issued that year. Also affixed to the front of the envelope is the Knockaloe Camp, I, of Man No. 866 Registration Etiquette, together with the Violet small type Aliens' Detention Camp Censored Knockaloe, I.O.M. Double Oval which is also known to be used in black and blue colours.

Bottom Right Pair: Left Hand Stamp:

The postcard printed within Knockaloe Camp and designed by an internee depicts the general layout of Knockaloe Camp together with a backdrop of a map of the Isle of Man, a Manx cat and emblem of the Three Legs of Man. It shows various buildings within the Camp and it sends "Greetings from the Prisoners at Knockaloe Camp, Peel, Isle of Man". This card is undated.

Right Hand Stamp:

This depicts the Internee-produced stamp from around 1916, believed to be sold for 2d and used, as this example indicates, on an internal Knockaloe mail sending i.e. from one camp to another. This cover is believed to have been sent by the actual designer of the stamp and it is thought that he designed the Knockaloe IOM Single Circle cancelling it.

ACKNOWLEDGEMENTS

The Isle of Man Post Office thanked everyone who provided assistance, guidance and permissions to reproduce artwork during the preparation of this stamp issue: Mr Kerry Kemp and Mannin Collections Limited.

Bibliography

The following publications have been of help in preparing this work and are recommended as further reading for those interested in the internee postal history of the Isle of Man:

Anon (1940) *Our Post Office*, Onchan Pioneer No 19, Pages 2-8.

Chappell, Connery (1984) *Island of Barbed Wire: Internment on the Isle of Man in World War Two*. London, Robert Hale Ltd, 1984 (reprinted 2005).

Cresswell, Yvonne M. (2010) *Living with the Wire: Civilian Internment in the Isle of Man during the two World Wars*. Douglas: Manx National Heritage, 2010, ISBN 978-0901106636. Revised and enlarged edition.

Field, Charles (1989) *Internment Mail of the Isle of Man*. Francis J. Field Ltd.

Francis, Paul (2006) *Isle of Man 20th Century Military. Archaeology Part 1: Island Defence*. Douglas: Manx Heritage Foundation. ISBN 10: 0954718062.

Giovannelli, Leonida N. (1971) *Paper Hero: At His Majesty's Pleasure: An Account of Life as a Manx Internee during World War II*. Douglas, Island Development Co. Ltd, 90 pages.

Isle of Man Examiner (1919), *Closure of Douglas Camp*, page 5, published 26th April 1919.

Kelly, Pat (1993) *Hedge of Thorns: Knockaloe Camp, 1915-1919*. Douglas: The Manx Experience. ISBN 1-873120-11-7.

Mark, Graham (2007) *Prisoners of War in British Hands during WWI, A study of their history, the camps and their mails*. Wiveliscombe, Postal History Society, 258 pages.

Osborne, Bernard G.F. (Ed.) (various) *Isle of Man Postal History Society Bulletin*.

Whitney, J.T. (1976) *Isle of Man Handbook of Stamps and Postal History*. Chippenham, Wiltshire: Picton Publishing & B.P.H. Publications Ltd. ISBN 0-902633-67-8.

Whitney, J.T. (1978) *Isle of Man Camp Mail - Manx Monographs #7*. Published J.T. Whitney.

Whitney, J.T. (1981) *Isle of Man Stamps and Postal History*. B.P.H. Publications, 309 pages. ISBN 10: 0-902633-67-8.

AFTERWORD

In addition to the bibliography earlier in this book, included here are other suggested areas of wider interest in the subjects dealt with in this publication. Additionally, those interested in the postal history of internment in the Isle of Man and who collect in this field of philately may come across items which are puzzling for one reason or another such as the one illustrated here. In this case it may be helpful to contact the Isle of Man Postal History Society which has been responsible for this publication.

A well-travelled cover unable to find the addressee.

The email address of the Secretary of this society, to whom queries should be addressed, is
iomphs@manx.net

Other sources suggested are listed below:

Books

Knockaloe Internment Camp Published Lily Publications Ltd, 2014	Rosalind Stimpson / Stephen Hall
Prisoners of Britain, German civilian and combatant internees during the First World War Published NBN International (Manchester University Press)	Panikos Panayi
This Terrible Ordeal Published Manx National Heritage 2013	Matthew Richardson
Island at War: The remarkable role played by the small Manx nation in the Great War 1914-18 Published Western Books, Laxey, IOM. 1986	Marjory West
A Military History of the Isle of Man Published T. Buncle & Co. Ltd. 1947	B. E. Sargeuant

The Isle of Man and the Great War Published Brown & Sons Ltd. Douglas, IOM. 1920	B. E. Sargeuant
Isle of Man Paper Money Published Pam West, British Notes, 2014	Pam West and Alan Kelly
Banknotes & Banking in the Isle of Man 1788-1994 Published Spink London 2nd Edition 1994	Ernest Quarmby
A Bespattered Page? – The Internment of His Majesty's Most Loyal Enemy Aliens Published Andre Deutsch Ltd. 1980	Ronald Stent
The Interment of Aliens in Twentieth Century Britain Published Frank Cass & Co. Ltd. London 1993	David Cesarani / Tony Kushner
Totally Un-English – Britain's Internment of Enemy Aliens in two World Wars Published Institute of Germanic & Romance Studies, University of London, 2005	Richard Dove
Die Mannerinfel (in German)	Dunbar Kalckreuth
Craftsmen and Quaker -The Story of James T. Baily 1876-1957	Leslie Baily
Occasions 13	Ernst Eisenmayer

Archives in the Isle of Man

Manx National Heritage Library, Manx Museum, Douglas.

Manx National Heritage, iMuseum, Douglas.

Leece Museum, The Quay, Peel.

Knockaloe and Patrick Visitors Centre.

Internet

http://www.knockaloe.org.uk/

http://www.knockaloe.im/

http://www.imuseum.im/

Appendix - Catalogue Numbers Compared

The two catalogues, one by Dr J. T. Whitney, which included a section on internee mail, and the other by Charles Field of internee mail, which are being updated in this publication have had numbers ascribed to various postmarks and cachets. For the postal historian who is in possession of these books the following chart may be of use in comparing marks already described with the new numbers allocated in this publication. Items which were not recorded in the earlier books are shown by the letter U, others are given the appropriate number or if differing slightly from those described are shown as "type". On occasions Dr J. T. Whitney did not give a number to the item but did illustrate it, in this case the page number in his book is given.

IOMPHS	Whitney	Field
100	649	1
101	649type	1type
101a	649type	1type
102	649type	1type
103	649type	1
104	649type	1type
105	U	U
106	U	U
107	U	U
108	U	U
109	U	U
110	Pg172/3	U
111	Pg172/3	U
112	Pg172/3	2
113	Pg172/3	9
114	Pg171	12
115	U	U
116	U	U
120	650	4
121	651	5
122	U	U
123	U	U
124	U	U
125	U	U
126	U	U
127	U	U
128	Pg173	7
129	Pg173	9
130	Pg173	8
131	Pg173	10
132	Pg173	10
140	645	15
141	645type	15type
142	645type	15type
143	645type	15type
144	645type	15type
145	645type	15type
146	646	16
147	646	16

IOMPHS	Whitney	Field
148	647	17
149	647type	17type
150	U	U
150a	U	U
151	644	11
152	Pg171	13
153	Pg171	12
154	Pg171	14
155	U	U
156	U	U
157	648	18
158	U	24
159	U	U
160	Pg243	25
160a	U	U
161	Pg172	20
162	Pg172	U
163	U	U
164	Pg172	19
165	Pg172	21
165a	U	21
166	U	U
167	U	U
168	Pg172	22
169	Pg172	23
170	Pg171	U
171	Pg171	3
172	U	U
173	U	U
174	U	U
175	U	U
176	U	U
177	U	U
178	U	U
179	U	U
180	U	U
181	U	U
182	U	U
183	U	U
184	U	U
185	U	U
186	U	U
187	U	U
188	U	U
189	U	U
190	U	U
201	652	26
202	653	27
203	Pg175	Pg6
203a	Pg175	Pg6
204	U	28
204a	U	U

IOMPHS	Whitney	Field
205	U	29
206	U	30
207	654	31
208	U	32
209	655	33
210	656	34
211	U	U
212	U	35
213	657	61
214	658	62
215	U	U
216	U	U
217	U	63
218	659	64
219	660	65
220	U	66
221	U	67
222	U	U
223	U	U
225	661	88
226	U	89
227	U	U
228	683type	90
230	662	84
231	U	U
235	663	74
236	U	75
237	U	U
238	U	U
239	U	76
240	U	U
241	U	U
242	U	U
242a	U	U
243	U	U
244	U	U
244a	U	U
245	664	73
246	644type	73type
247	U	U
248	U	U
250	665	51
251	665A	52
252	U	U
253	665B	53
254	667	56
255	666	54
256	668	55
257	U	58
258	U	U
259	669	60
260	U	U

IOMPHS	Whitney	Field
261	U	U
262	U	Pg10
262a	U	U
263	U	U
264	U	U
265	670	68
266	671(2)	69
267	671	70
268	U	71
268a	U	71type
269	U	U
270	U	72
275	U	U
276	672	85
277	U	U
278	U	U
279	673	36
280	674	37
280a	674type	37type
281	674type	37type
282	U	U
283	U	38
284	U	U
285	U	U
286	U	U
287	U	U
288	U	U
289	U	U
290	U	U
291	675	77
292	U	78
293	676	79
294	677	80
295	U	81
296	U	83
297	Pg181	82type
297m	U	82type
297x	Pg181	82
298	U	U
299	U	U
300	U	U
301	U	U
302	U	U
303	U	U
304	U	U
305	U	U
305a	U	U
306	U	86
307	U	87
310	678	41
311	679	42
312	680	43

IOMPHS	Whitney	Field
313	682	47
314	U	U
314a	U	48
315	U	U
316	U	44
317	U	45
318	681	46
319	U	49
320	U	U
321	683	50
322	683type	50type
323	U	U
324	Pg183	U
325	Pg183	U
326	U	U
326a	U	U
350	U	U
351	U	91
352	U	92
353	U	93
354	U	94
360	U	U
361	U	U
362	U	U
363	U	U
365	U	U
366	U	U
367	U	U
368	U	U
369	U	U
370	U	U

Index

Zurich d/ rect h/s 23 x 15 mm WW1   21, 22

We acknowledge permission to reproduce postcards from the Private Collection of Peter Daniel, son of the late Lt. Col. Daniel who, as Captain H. O. Daniel opened, as its first commander, Hutchinson Internment Camp in 1940.

Kriegs-Gefangenen Lager

Entwurf, Stahlstich und Druck im Lager ausgeführt.

Zur Unterstützung der Bestrebungen der Kranken